Archpriest Alexei Uminsky

THE DIVINE LITURGY

An Explanation of Its Meaning and Content for Laity

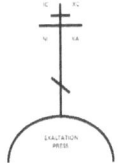

Grand Rapids - Exaltation Press - 2021

Copyright © 2021 Exaltation Press

Author: Archpriest Alexei Uminsky
Translator: Fr. John Hogg

"The Divine Liturgy - An explanation of its meaning and content for laity"

Fr. Alexei Uminsky is the rector of the Church of the Life-giving Trinity in Moscow and the author of many books. This book is his first to appear in English. It was originally given as a series of lectures. In it, Fr. Alexei breaks down the meaning and content of the Liturgy in a way that is both detailed and accessible. Since the Divine Liturgy and the Eucharist are at the center of our life as Christians, it is our hope that this book will help in the development of a deeper appreciation of the Divine Services of the Orthodox Church, a deeper connection to the Church, and most importantly, a deeper love of Christ.

All rights reserved. This book or any portion thereof may not be reproduced or used in any manner whatsoever without the express written permission of the publisher except for the use of brief quotations in a book review.

Translated from the original "Божественная Литургия: Объяснение смысла, значения, содержания" by Nikea Press, Copyright © Trading house «NIKEA», www.Nikeabooks.ru

ISBN: 978-1-950067-04-6 (Paperback)

Edited by Pauline Harris
With thanks to Al Blazek and Cindy Hogg

First printing edition 2021.

Exaltation Press
Grand Rapids, MI

www.ExaltationPress.com

For bulk orders, please contact editor@exaltationpress.com

TABLE OF CONTENTS

1 LITURGY AS THE CENTER OF CHRISTIAN LIFE	5
2 THE EUCHARIST IN THE EARLY CHRISTIAN CHURCH	11
3 THE GATHERING OF THE CHURCH	17
4 PRIESTLY VESTMENTS	27
5 THE SACRED VESSELS	33
6 HOW THE PROSKOMEDIA WAS FORMED	37
7 THE PROSKOMEDIA	43
8 LITURGY AS THE MYSTERY OF THE KINGDOM	53
9 THE PETITIONS OF THE GREAT LITANY	57
10 THE ANTIPHONS	69
11 THE TRISAGION HYMN	77
12 THE EPISTLE READING	81
13 THE GOSPEL READING	85
14 THE LITANY OF FERVENT SUPPLICATION	91
15 THE LITANY OF THE CATECHUMENS	95
16 THE CHERUBIC HYMN	101
17 THE SYMBOL OF FAITH - THE NICENE CREED	109
18 THE EUCHARISTIC CANON	115
19 PREPARATION FOR COMMUNION - THE LORD'S PRAYER	135
20 AFTER THE LORD'S PRAYER: HOLY THINGS ARE FOR THE HOLY	153
21 COMMUNION OF THE CLERGY AND FAITHFUL	157
22 THANKSGIVING	165

1
LITURGY AS THE CENTER OF CHRISTIAN LIFE

All Church feasts would lose their meaning if not for Pascha. For if Christ had not risen, then all the other events in the Gospels could only be looked at in their historical context. They would not have any value, except in a moral and cultural sense. We say that every Christian feast belongs to eternity in as much as it is spiritually filled with Pascha. Eternity is present here in our time, and we become real participants of the feast.

The same thing can be said about Liturgy, which towers above all the other Divine Services. If there were no Liturgy, then it would be completely pointless to serve any of the other services because without Liturgy, there would be no Church as such.

And so, any discussion about the Eucharist (from the Greek word ευχαριστία—thanksgiving) must take place in tandem with a discussion about what exactly the Church is and how the Church and the Eucharist are connected to each other.

* * *

When we come to Holy Baptism, whether as an adult or an infant, the priest asks us or our sponsors, "Do you believe in God? Have you united yourself to Christ?" and we answer that yes, we have united ourselves to Christ and that yes, we believe in Him as King and God. Thus, we pledge ourselves to serve the Lord.

Immediately after our answer, we read the Symbol of Faith, the Creed, which lists exactly what it is that we believe. In part, the Symbol of Faith contains the following words: "I believe in one holy, catholic, and apostolic Church." This is essential to understand—along with faith in God, we also confess faith in the Church. No other religious system besides Christianity has this same understanding of "faith in the Church." The catechism of St. Philaret Drozdov (1782/83 – 1867) defines the Church as "the community of people who are united by the same faith and the same rites." However, the same thing could be said about any religious association, for example, the Muslim or Jewish communities. You can belong to the community and take part in carrying out its rites which come from the tenants of its faith, but it is impossible to have faith in the community. None of these communities are for their members what the Church is for Christians.

And so what exactly does it mean "to have faith in the Church?" We are not confessing an obligation to go to church on Sundays and feast days. We are not promising God that we will keep the fasts, that we will go to Confession and take Communion. For

Christians, the Church is not just a place where they can commune with God, because they can do that at home, in the subway, in the forest, in any place and at any time. To "have faith in the Church" means to confess that it is the Body of Christ, of which you and I are members. The Apostle Paul writes about the Church, saying, "For just as the body is one and has many members, and all the members of the body, though many, are one body, so it is with Christ. For in one Spirit we were all baptized into one body" (1 Cor. 12:12-13). He later adds "you are the body of Christ and individually members of it" (1 Cor. 12:27).

A part of the body that has been cut off cannot live independently. When we talk about the Church as a living organism, we are talking about a united and indivisible body in which the human and divine are joined together. The Church is the mystical gathering of people where the union of God and man takes places and where a united divine and human organism is born.

We come to church in order to become a part of it, to become its essence, its nature. The Church joins our nature to Christ because we are the body of the Church and He is its Head. For this reason, as a recent Serbian saint, the great theologian Justin Popovich, said, the Church itself is the God-man Jesus Christ. It is us with Christ. In such a case, it becomes clear that simply being present in Church and fulfilling a few external rules, simply knowing certain dogmas, is clearly not enough. Instead, we are talking about a way of life that Orthodox Christians call faith. Christ teaches us, "I am the Way, the Truth, and the Life" (John 14:6). The same thing can be said about the Church. The Church is the way, the Church is the truth, the Church is man's life in faith and as such is the meaning of Christianity.

Finally, we do not believe only in the *existence* of God, that the Lord is a Person who created the world, that there is a certain relationship between Him and man, that there are certain rules that should be followed, as we await a reward for our deeds after death. All religious beliefs, even the most primitive, have these characteristics in common. This is not the meaning of the Christian faith. Our hope is us being saved in eternal life by being united to God. Eternal life *is* abiding in God, being united to Him; it is the deification of man, as he becomes god. Without resorting to complex theological definitions, this is the true meaning of the Christian faith.

The Church makes us share in God's nature. The Apostle Peter writes about this: "His divine power has granted to us all things that pertain to life and godliness, through the knowledge of him who called us to his own glory and excellence, by which he has granted to us his precious and very great promises, so that through them you may become partakers of the Divine Nature" (2 Peter 1:3-4). We often do not notice these words but they contain the essence of all the Apostolic epistles. We must become partakers of the Divine Nature. St. Seraphim of Sarov said the same thing in a slightly different way: "We must acquire the Holy Spirit."

The point of the Christian life is to be filled with the Holy Spirit, to become of the same nature as the Lord, to be united to Him. If this happens, then our time here on Earth becomes meaningful and our life becomes truly spiritual.

This is precisely the meaning of the Church—

that in any other way, man is not capable of reaching God. This is why Christ founded His Church on Earth, through which man receives grace, the knowledge of God, and communion with Him. However, it is essential to make one clarification. For man, a full knowledge of God will always remain unobtainable since the Lord is absolute, unending, and eternal, while man is by nature created. Our communion with God does not touch His Divine Essence, which man will never be able to partake in. God became man in all of His fullness but man becomes a son of God by grace. It is grace that makes us into a god-man because the Lord gives us the ability to partake of His Flesh and Blood. This is given to us through the great Mystery of the Church, through our life in it, because Christ Himself said, "Whoever is thirsty, let him come to me and drink" (John 7:37)

2
THE EUCHARIST IN THE EARLY CHRISTIAN CHURCH

The goal of our talks is to explain how connected the Christian spiritual life is to the Eucharist. Is it possible to live a spiritual life outside of the Eucharist or only communing once in awhile? In order to answer these questions we need to understand exactly what the Eucharist was for the early Christian Church, the state of our Divine Services today, and finally, discern as much as possible what participation in the Divine Liturgy means for us personally.

The first time the Eucharist was celebrated was at the Mystical Supper by the Savior before His sufferings on the Cross. "Jesus took bread, and after blessing it broke it and gave it to the disciples, and said, 'Take, eat; this is My Body.' And He took a cup, and when He had given thanks He gave it to them, saying, 'Drink of it, all of you, for this is My Blood of the covenant, which is poured out for many for the forgiveness of sins'" (Matthew 26:26-28). The Lord gave this commandment to the apostles and to all of us as well. "Do this in remembrance of Me" (Luke 22:19). The focus of every Liturgy is the remembrance of that very Mystical Supper that we are living through. In a mystical way, we enter into eternity and become real participants of this event.

In the book of Acts, we find a description of the Eucharist. During the first period of Christianity, the Divine Services in which Communion was celebrated were called by different names but the most common names were "the breaking of the bread" and "the Eucharist." Today, the word "Eucharist" is commonly used to refer to the Liturgy, especially since the Liturgy has at its core the Eucharistic Canon.

The apostles gathered in various homes with their disciples in order to break bread. The first Christians were traditional Jews and regularly visited the Temple of Jerusalem up until its destruction in AD 70 by the Roman emperor Titus. The worship services practiced there at the time were still something that connected early Christian communities at the beginning.

However, in spite of the fact that worship continued in the Temple of Jerusalem, the Apostolic Church had already separated itself from it and little by little, Christian gatherings moved into communities headed by the apostles.

What were these gatherings like? At the time, there was still no written Gospel, but its oral form had already become an integral part of Holy Tradition. The apostles talked about Christ, about "that which was from the beginning, which we have heard, which we have seen with our eyes, which we looked upon and have touched with our hands" (1 John 1:1). They shared this invaluable experience of having been God's companions generously with new converts. During these gatherings, the apostles told the story of Jesus: His birth, baptism, sermons, the miracles He had done, and the legacy He had left behind.

We know that after his sermon, the Apostle Peter at first baptized 3,000 and later another 5,000 adult men, very impressive figures for those times—about the population of a whole city. When they told the story of Christ, it was the "Good News" that would later be written down by the four Evangelists and canonized by the Church as Holy Scripture.

In order to show that their assertions were well founded, the apostles read from the Old Testament prophecies which bore witness to the fact that Christ is the true Son of God and that every one of His actions corresponded to what was foretold in the Old Testament. After that, the apostles' own epistles to the communities they had already founded were read. At this point, we are talking not about the very first years, but rather the first decades of Christianity when the apostles, preaching the Gospel to the world, traveled the whole Earth. In many major cities they had founded communities that made up autocephalous, or administratively independent, Churches. These Churches passed the Apostolic epistles from one community to another as precious testimonies of the Truth.

Only after the whole community had been nourished by the word of God was it time for another Word to come—the Incarnate Word. Even today, we call the first part of the Liturgy, the Liturgy of the Catechumens, the "Liturgy of the Word." But a "word" is not just a means of expressing a human thought. In the Holy Scriptures, God Himself is called "the Word!"

An Apostle would take the bread and wine that had been brought and celebrate the Eucharist, "thanksgiving," in memory of the Mystical Supper. He would read prayers of thanksgiving for all of the Lord's mercy that He has sent down on the world. But most of all, he would give thanks for the blessings that had taken place before the apostles' own eyes: how God became flesh and walked on Earth, how He took on Himself the sins of the whole world, ascended the Cross and redeemed all of humanity by His sufferings, how He rose from the dead and ascended into Heaven and sent the Holy Spirit on His disciples.

The Eucharistic prayer includes thanksgiving for the creation of the world, for God's saving providence for the world, and for the Second Coming and God's eternal Kingdom. In other words, Apostolic thanksgiving was always connected with eternity, including in equal measure a remembrance of what had already happened, a testimony of what currently is and a prophecy about that which must come to pass.

The Apostle would then ask the Holy Spirit to come to this community of saints and sanctify the gifts that had been brought, the bread and wine, and make them the true Body and Blood of Christ. In our day, as well, the Church does the same, giving thanks for the gifts of the Holy Spirit.

After this, the Bread was broken and given to all who were present. The people then went to the Chalice and communed of the same Word, but no longer in a spoken, but Incarnate, way and they all became that Word. That is why the Book of Acts says that "the Word of God grew" (Acts 6:7).

Returning home after the Eucharistic gathering,

every Christian was the word of God that was spoken to the world. That is why the Church began to be called "Apostolic."

3
THE GATHERING OF THE CHURCH

Reading the writings of the Apostolic fathers, for example, of St. Irenaeus of Lyons or St. Ignatius the God-bearer, we notice that more than once, the authors emphasize that "Where the bishop is, there is the Apostolic Church." The church community, headed by a bishop, was a local Church. These Churches existed in almost every polis. At the same time, however, there still were not many Christians. According to the rules at the time, a bishop could be given to a community that had at least twelve people in it.

From the very beginning of the spread of Christianity, it was established that the only true celebrant of Liturgy was a bishop because he was the one who headed the Church. That is how things were for the first three centuries. Liturgy in the ancient Church was conciliar. Usually, each city had only one Liturgy because there was only one bishop there. As we read in the Book of Acts, "all who believed were together" (Acts 2:44). Liturgy was always served on Sunday at dawn, in memory of Christ's resurrection. At the time, Sunday was not a day off since the pagan world lived according to a completely different calendar. And of course, it was unimaginable that someone might come to Liturgy and not commune. After all, that was why they had gathered. The Divine Service itself preceded the communion of the faithful in the Holy Mysteries of Christ. It was an introduction, a spiritual preparation for the celebration of the Mystery.

Not all Christians were able to come to the Sunday service every time. For that reason, it was not uncommon for them to take Communion home with them as reserved Gifts. Priests were not the only ones who could commune the faithful. Deacons and deaconesses[1] were able to as well. Additionally, according to the tradition of the time, after each Liturgy a Christian would take home a portion of the Holy Gifts and begin each day by communing of the Holy Mysteries of Christ.

Afterward, when Christianity began to spread throughout the empire and became, thanks to the Holy Emperor Constantine the Great, the Equal-to-the-Apostles (272-337), the religion of the state, priests became the bishop's concelebrants, although they were only able to fill in for the bishop when he was off on diocesan business or was imprisoned or in exile. The bishop could entrust a priest with serving Liturgy in his place, but this was an exception rather

---

1   This special form of ministry, which should not be viewed as part of Holy Orders, existed in the early Church. Pious widows who lived near the Church were given the blessing of the bishop to take the Holy Gifts to prisons and hospitals and to give them to those who were suffering. They also baptized women and were allowed to take communion in the Altar.

than the rule.

Only after parish churches began to be opened were priests given certain episcopal functions: a degree of independence in the administration of their small communities and, most importantly, permission at first to serve Liturgy and then later on, Chrismation as well.

As a sign of their blessing, bishops sent priests *antimensia* that they had signed, which were cloth boards with a piece of relics sewn in them as a reminder that the first Liturgies were served on the tombs of the martyrs. Modern antimensia usually depict Christ being laid in the tomb. In terms of their outward appearance, shape, and inscription, they are like the *epitaphios* which is brought out on Holy Saturday to be reverenced.

Even now, without an antimension signed by a bishop, a priest cannot serve Liturgy in any circumstances whatsoever since he serves exclusively at the bishop's blessing and by himself has no such authority. A priest is the bishop's assistant, his concelebrant. And the priest's concelebrants are all the rest of the parishioners.

* * *

Liturgy begins with everyone assembling together. The word "Church" itself in Greek is *ecclesia*, which in turn means "an assembly."

The Apostle Paul explains what it means to assemble for Liturgy. In his day, there were no church buildings. Christians gathered for the Eucharist in houses, in the catacombs, and in other secret places. That is why the Apostle's words "when you come together as a Church" (1 Cor. 11:18) should not be interpreted as "when you get ready to go to a church building." When we assemble in church, we also assemble together *as the Church*, the same Church that we confess our belief in.

Our Eucharistic assembly is an assembly in Christ which is essential for us to be able to be united to God and through God to be united deeply and eternally with each other. Strictly speaking, such an assembly of people in the Mystery actually makes the people into the Church. Once, the priest arrived at church when the whole community was already assembled. Today, unfortunately, he quite often arrives to find an empty church, reads his Entrance Prayers and vests in silence. Only a reader is there at the choir stand, waiting for his blessing to begin reading the Hours. However, the priest should be coming to the Church, that is, to the community of people that he will be heading, to the community that is called "the people of God." The Apostle Peter wrote about this people, "you yourselves like living stones are being built up as a spiritual house, to be a holy priesthood, to offer spiritual sacrifices acceptable to God through Jesus Christ. For it stands in Scripture: 'Behold, I am laying in Zion a stone, a cornerstone chosen and precious, and whoever believes in him will not be put to shame'" (1 Peter 2:5-6).

Pay attention to how the Bible uses the word "stone." The Devil invites Christ to turn stones into bread: "And the tempter came and said to him, 'If you are the Son of God, command these stones to become loaves of bread'" (Matthew 4:3). John the Baptist accuses the Pharisees and Sadducees, saying: "And do not presume to say to yourselves, 'We have Abraham as our father,' for I tell you, God is able from these stones to raise up children for Abraham" (Matthew 3:9). And Christ speaks to His Apostle, saying, "You are Peter, and on this rock I will build my Church, and the gates of hell shall not prevail against it. I will give you the keys of the Kingdom of Heaven, and whatever you bind on Earth shall be bound in Heaven, and whatever you loose on Earth shall be loosed in Heaven" (Matthew 16:18-19). And during the Divine Services, we often hear the words, "The stone that the builders rejected has become the cornerstone" (Psalm 117:22 LXX).

It might seem like nothing could be more dead than a stone, right? Even wood is more alive. At one time it was a tree that grew, flowered, and sprouted leaves. But here we have a paradox—a living stone . A stone is strong and inherently the same and unchanging from age to age. You can lean on it, build on it. Nevertheless, stones are without feeling and lifeless from eternity. We can sometimes be similar. There is a spiritual concept—stoniness of heart.

And then suddenly, a living stone, with the breath of life, immortal. This is Christ, who holds everything in His hand, which is why he is called the *Pantocrator*[2]. He is the stone which the builders refused but which has become the chief cornerstone.

The devil invited God to turn stones into bread because the tempter always suggests temptations that are in essence frauds and deceptions but simultaneously resemble the truth. For the Lord actually does make bread out of stones. He does take what is lifeless and

---

2   "Pantocrator," a word meaning "Almighty," contains the Greek root "κρατάω," meaning "I hold," with the prefix "παντ-" meaning everything, so "the one who holds all things."

make it alive. He does raise up children of Abraham out of stones. The Apostle Peter tells us, "You yourselves like living stones, build out of yourselves a spiritual house, a holy priesthood, to offer spiritual sacrifices acceptable to God through Jesus Christ" (1 Peter 2:5).

We are the stones from which He can raise up children of Abraham. And when we commune of the Body and Blood of Christ, we are made alive and we become partakers of the Bread of Life and are joined to Him and become Living Stones and build out of ourselves a spiritual house—the Church of God. Peter was told "on this rock I will build my Church, and the gates of hell shall not prevail against it" (Matthew 16:18). Each of us, each Christian, needs to understand: We also are stones. We also are "Peters." We are the temple of God, the Church of the Living God. But this is only possible if we are living stones, and not dead ones. And we receive life from the Savior.

The Lord makes us living stones and we, like architects, take part in building up the house of God. If we build God's spiritual house out of ourselves that means that each of must put his spiritual life on the foundation of the Church. The Church is built on the desire of the people to be the body of Christ, to become those living stones.

* * *

Pay attention to these words: "Build out of yourselves a spiritual house, a holy priesthood." It turns out that we do not only need to carry the temple within ourselves but we also need to be its priest. You yourself—be both a receptacle of God, a place where God abides and also serve him as priest within that temple. A priest is one who serves the Divine Services.

How does a priest serve God? He celebrates the Mysteries and brings sacrifices to the Lord. The first sacrifice is a broken spirit. The second is a sacrifice of praise: "Let everything that has breath praise the Lord."

A priest is a person dedicated to God, building a house for God out of himself. He dedicates all of himself to God—all of his intentions, all of his feelings, and all of his actions. That is a holy priesthood.

In a different place, the Apostle says, "But you are a chosen race, a royal priesthood, a holy nation, a people for his own possession ... Once you were not a people, but now you are God's people" (1 Peter 2:9-10). Pay attention to these amazing words! What are they telling us? That all of us who are assembled in the Church are a special people, the people of God, that carry within ourselves the marks of the kingdom and of the priesthood because the Lord Himself who makes us His body is the king of Earth and Heaven, and the High Priest.

"The people of God" is not just those who believe. Rather, it is the Church which unites us all and makes us into a new people. One theologian said that the Church is a holy nation, a nation chosen by God. There used to be a God-chosen nation that the Lord set apart to make it His own, to call that people His son: "Out of Egypt I called my son" (Matthew 2:15).

At first, these words prophesied about all the Jews Moses led out of Egypt. However, these God-chosen people rejected the stone on which they stood and so God chose a new people—a people in whom He sees more than just individuals who physically resemble each other and speak the same language, and He calls them "a royal priesthood." This people communes with the Savior who offered Himself as a sacrifice to His Father for the whole world. That is His high priesthood.

Each of us is given what He Himself possesses. First, His name, since we are Christians. Second, the signs that He, as King and Priest, gives to us all—His Kingdom and His priesthood. In any one of us, the Lord sees a priest and a king because we as a people are born again in the Mystery of Holy Baptism and Chrismation, receiving the seal of the Holy Spirit.

There is a world that is separated from the Church and not sanctified and there is a world within the Church. And so in the world of the Church, we are all priests. The first order of the priesthood that each of us is consecrated into during Baptism and Chrismation is the rank of the laity. Every Orthodox Christian has been consecrated into this order.

* * *

But it is not uncommon that people who come to the Church and bring with them their griefs and infirmities at the same time do not end up becoming *the Church*. They come, pay some money, and leave, and the Church, they say, is praying for us. By Church, of course, they mean above all the priest who by himself, without the people of God, does not have the power of prayer that the true, catholic Church possesses.

When you and I assemble together in the temple of God to become the Church, we gather to serve the Lord, to be the priests of the temple along with the priest that the Church, through the bishop, has appointed to head the assembly. The Divine Services are our common prayer.

"Liturgy" ("λειτουργία") when translated from Greek means "a common work." In the ancient world, the act of building a temple or a ship was called "liturgy." People gathered together and all together undertook a work that they would not have been able to do without everyone participating. The Russian word for "laity," *miryane*, comes from the word for "world," in other words, from this understanding of the "whole world" working together. And so you can say that in a temple, all the people are concelebrants. The people are not a mute flock, separated from the priests by a wall, but are rather a united people of God, including the bishop, the clergy, and the laity.

There is a priestly hierarchy which is headed by the bishops, followed by the priests, then the deacons, and then the laity. Along with the grace of Baptism we receive also the grace of priesthood toward the rest of the world. That is why we speak of concelebration and say that in the temple the people gather to serve together. It should not be the case that the priest serves Liturgy, and the parishioners only light candles and write lists of people to be prayed for. All of us should serve God together with united lips and hearts, praising and glorifying Him, united to each other in the unbreakable unity of faith, in unity of love, and in the unity of good thoughts and deeds. We are called to offer up our prayers for everyone. It was not for nothing that the Lord said, "where two or three are gathered in my name, there am I among them" (Matthew 18:20). The people who are gathered together in the name of the Lord become the Body of Christ and then the prayer of the Church acquires enormous importance and power.

In the Book of Acts, we read that when Jacob and Peter were freed from prison and the apostles gathered to pray together, the Earth shook from their prayers. The prayer of the Church cannot but be heard, cannot but be fulfilled. The prayer of the Church has an all-powerful quality to it and unites man with God. Then the promise is fulfilled: "If you ask me anything in my name, I will do it" (John 14:14).

The priest in the Altar offers a visible sacrifice—the gifts that stand on the Throne (the table that stands in the Altar opposite the Royal Doors and which has been blessed by a bishop so that Liturgy can be served on it). The laity also offer a sacrificial service—they serve the Lord by taking up their crosses and carrying them, sharing misfortunes and grief in common. And then the next step is our common participation in the Holy Mysteries of Christ.

4
PRIESTLY VESTMENTS

A priest's entrance into the temple is accompanied by Entrance Prayers that he reads, while still not vested, before the Royal Doors, piously asking God to give him the strength he needs to serve. He asks God to strengthen him for the upcoming service and to cleanse him from his sins so that he can serve the Mystery without condemnation. He prays the following: "Stretch forth Thy hand, O Lord, from Thy holy dwelling-place on high, and strengthen me for this, Thine appointed service; that standing uncondemned before Thy dread Throne, I may fulfill the sacred, bloodless sacrifice, for Thine is the power and the glory unto ages of ages. Amen."

Afterward, the priest asks for forgiveness from anyone who is in the temple at that moment and then goes into the Altar while reading the Psalm, "I shall enter into Thy house ..." makes three bows before the Throne, and then vests while reading prayers which reveal the meaning of his priestly clothing.

At the beginning, the clergy did not have special

clothing, but over time they were given certain external signs that distinguished them from other members of the Church. The vestments of deacons, priests, and bishops are similar in many ways. A deacon's vestments consist of his stikharion, orarion, and cuffs. In addition to these things, he also has an epitrachelion (an orarion folded in two), a belt, and a phelonion.

All of the specific details of the clerical vestments came to us from Byzantium and have symbolic meaning. As the priest puts them on, he reads prayers which explain the meaning of each piece of the vestments.

As the priest puts on his *stikharion*, he remembers the incorruptibility of Baptism through which people have put on Christ. The stikharion looks like a white shirt and signifies chastity and purity, the wedding garments in which the Lord waits for us at His wedding feast. The bride of Christ is the Church and the Church is you and I. By putting on snow-white clothing before the beginning of Liturgy, the priest personifies the wedding between the Church and Christ. He enters the Altar as the representative of the people of God. He is not separated from the people who have assembled in the temple. Rather, he comes before God as the head of the people.

The cuffs (both the deacon's and the priest's) are worn as a sign that it is not by their own strength, by their own hands, their own power, or reasoning that they serve the Divine Services but rather by the power of God and His mercy. He cannot do anything if his hands are not filled with divine grace.

As he puts on the belt, the priest prays, "Blessed is God who girds me with strength ." The belt symbolizes a readiness to be obedient and serve.

The priest is ready to go wherever God shows him, to pay attention to all of His commands, and to hear His call. The priest has to be a warrior of Christ!

Instead of a deacon's *orarion*, a priest wears an *epitrachelion*, which symbolizes the grace of the priesthood. An epitrachelion looks like a yoke that is used to harness oxen or horses. The Apostle Paul warns us, "You shall not muzzle an ox when it treads out the grain" (1 Cor. 9:9). An ox walks in a circle and turns the millstone. He threshes grain and this, too, is a Eucharistic image. By vesting, the priest promises God that he will work diligently for Him. The epitrachelion expresses that the priest will work his field like an ox that has been harnessed.

But this "yoke" that is put on him is the yoke of grace. And this grace is not light or joyful. It is, however, the grace about which Christ says "My yoke is good" (Matthew 11:30). None of the services are done without the priest wearing his epitrachelion.

Finally, the priest vests in his *phelonion*, or *chasuble*, which symbolizes the glory of the Church, her purity and holiness, and the grace that fills her which covers all human shortcomings, weaknesses, and internal defects. The priest puts on this robe of truth like armor that protects him from all hostile powers. Then he washes his hands which symbolizes the purity of his soul and life.

A deacon's stikharion and cuffs have the same meaning as those of a priest. When he vests in them, he says the same prayers that the priest does.

The word "orarion" dates back to the Latin verb "orare" which means "to pray." The deacon uses his orarion to call the parishioners to prayer. The orarion symbolizes the wings an angel has on its back.

If you pay attention, you will notice that angels are depicted on icons wearing the vestments of a deacon, a stikharion and orarion. The angels pray ceaselessly and ceaselessly glorify God, and a deacon's ministry of prayer is like the ministry of the ranks of angels.

A bishop's vestments also include a stikharion, epitrachelion, belt, and cuffs. The sakkos, which takes the place of the phelonion, is like a deacon's stikharion, only wider and shorter. It has the same meaning as a priest's phelonion. The *omophorion* symbolizes the lost sheep and reminds us that the bishop's ministry consists of bringing each lost sheep to Christ.

The bishop's staff symbolizes how the Church on Earth is like a wanderer that has no fixed place but rather is always on the path to the Kingdom of Heaven since only there do we find our true homeland, our true fatherland.

The mitre which is placed on the bishop's head personifies Christ's crown of thorns because the Church which the bishop governs, in the words of Patriarch Alexei I, is the Body of Christ, which is always being broken, always being subject to mocking, spitting, and crucifixion.

* * *

For us as Orthodox Christians, all of the symbolism in the temple building is very important. At the same time, it is not absolute. We need to understand its temporal, historical nature and meaning. And so, for example, if a member of the clergy is not wearing his vestments at a particular moment, he does not cease to be a member of the clergy because of that. In prison and in concentration camps, priests did not have any vestments with them but still served the Mysteries. In the ancient world, a "symbol" was a clay or wooden stamp that would be split in half when two friends would part. Each of them would then keep their half as a sign of their faithfulness and unity. A "symbol," then, was a sign of what unites people and makes them into a single whole.

Today the word "symbol" usually means a depiction of something that is not actually there in reality. A symbol plays a kind of artificial, almost theatrical, role. For example, in some books on liturgics, we read that during the Little Entrance, the priest "depicts" Christ coming to preach. This later symbolism tends to obscure what is going on rather than explain it. In a certain sense, it profanes all that is sacred, mysterious, and awe-inspiring, which cannot be described or explained with words but can only be a manifestation of power and Spirit.

Really, no one is "depicting" anything. Liturgy, rather, is supposed to reveal! Any Church symbol reveals reality and presence and certainly does not replace absence. So, if an icon was a symbol that replaced Christ, it would quickly become an idol.

The symbols that are present in Liturgy are there as signs of what is inexplicable but real because words are not sufficient to reveal the reality of what is taking place. Symbols help us in the same way that parables do.

5
THE SACRED VESSELS

The Chalice and Diskos are the most important vessels for the Divine Services, which were already used by the Savior Himself during the Mystical Supper. The *Diskos* (in Greek, "δίσκος") is a plate on a stand with a depiction of scenes from the New Testament, usually an icon of the Nativity of Christ. The Diskos simultaneously symbolizes the cave of Bethlehem and the Lord's tomb.

The two cross-shaped covers that cover the Chalice and Diskos and a square of fabric called the aer on the one hand symbolize the swaddling blankets that the Savior was wrapped in at His Nativity and on the other hand, the burial shroud he was wrapped in after He was taken down from the Cross.

The communion spoon is a small spoon with a long handle which is used to commune the laity. It did not appear until later on and became entrenched in Liturgical practice fairly late. It reminds us about the prophecy from Isaiah: "Then one of the seraphim flew to me, having in his hand a burning coal that he had taken with tongs from the Altar. And he touched my mouth and said: 'Behold, this has touched your lips; your guilt is taken away, and your sin atoned for'" (Isaiah 6:6-7). This is an Old Testament image of Communion. The spoon symbolizes the tongs with which the archangel pulled the coal out of the fire.

On the Cross, the Savior was pierced with the spear of a Roman soldier. During Liturgy, a sharp knife, which is called "the Spear," is used to cut out the Lamb and take out particles from the loaves of prosphora.

The Star, which is made in the shape of a cross, simultaneously represents the crucifixion and the Star of Bethlehem which showed the Magi the way to the Savior when He was born into the world.

When serving Liturgy, we must use red grape wine mixed with a small bit of hot water (the *Zeon*). This follows the example of the Lord, who, during the Mystical Supper, used wine mixed with water. It also calls to mind the blood and water which flowed out from the Savior's side when He was pierced by a spear while suffering on the Cross.

In Orthodox worship, we use leavened wheat bread baked in a form called prosphora (from the Ancient Greek word "προσφορά," meaning "offering"). Prosphora is round and in the Russian tradition is made out of two parts as a sign of how the Lord Jesus Christ has both a divine and a human nature but one divine-human Person. The upper part of the prosphora loaf should be stamped with an image of a cross. On either side of the upper part of the Cross, there are the letters "IC" and "XC," which stand for the name of the Savior ("*ΙΗΣΟΥΣ ΧΡΙΣΤΟΣ*" in Greek).

On either side of the lower part of the Cross are the letters "NIKA," which means "victory" in Greek. An image of the Mother of God or of the saints can also be present on the prosphora loaf.

In the Russian tradition, five prosphora loaves are used for the Liturgy of St. John Chrysostom. In addition, the priest uses a large number of small prosphora loaves to take out particles to commemorate the living and departed, from prayer lists written down by the faithful.

Not all of these practices appeared right away. In ancient times, the Service of Proskomedia did not exist in the form that we have it now. It solidified only near the end of the first millennium. In the Book of Acts, Liturgy was called "the breaking of the Bread." When the apostles served Liturgy or when it was served in the catacombs during times of persecution, only two sacred vessels were used for the Proskomedia—the Chalice and the Diskos, on which the broken Body of Christ was set out. The faithful took the Body from the Diskos and drank together from the Chalice. In other words, they communed the same way that priests do now in the Altar. Later on, during the reign of Constantine, the Church grew significantly, and parish temples began to appear and it became difficult to break the Bread for so many communicants. The Spear and Spoon appeared for the first time during the time of St. John Chrysostom (ca. AD 347-407).

In our worship, nothing exists by itself. All of these accessories serve to provide a fuller sense of the meaning of the Mystery that is taking place.

6
HOW THE PROSKOMEDIA WAS FORMED

The order of the Divine Liturgy can be divided up into three parts: the Proskomedia, the Liturgy of the Catechumens, and the Liturgy of the Faithful. First, let us talk about how the Proskomedia service came to be. At a basic level, the point of the Proskomedia is the preparation of the elements needed to serve the Mystery out of the bread and wine which have been brought to the temple. During this service, all the members of the Church—both on Earth and in Heaven—are commemorated.

The word "*Proskomedia*" (προσκομιδή) is a Greek word which means something that is brought or offered. In the community of the Holy apostles, each Christian had their "offering," an offering like the movement of the soul, like the meaning of the gathering, like something that united all the people. They all considered everything to be held in common. This is a very important sign. First, as the Book of Acts emphasizes that all of the people had "a common heart." Second, nobody considered anything to be his own. Third, each person brought what could serve the common good.

The sixth chapter of Acts talks about the election of seven deacons and their ordination to a special ministry, that of "distributing what was needed." The fifth chapter recounts the story of Ananias and Sapphira. This story causes some people a lot of confusion. Let us recall what happens:

> "A man named Ananias, with his wife Sapphira, sold a piece of property, and with his wife's knowledge he kept back for himself some of the proceeds and brought only a part of it and laid it at the apostles' feet. But Peter said, 'Ananias, why has Satan filled your heart to lie to the Holy Spirit and to keep back for yourself part of the proceeds of the land? While it remained unsold, did it not remain your own? And after it was sold, was it not at your disposal? Why is it that you have contrived this deed in your heart? You have not lied to man but to God.' When Ananias heard these words, he fell down and breathed his last. And great fear came upon all who heard of it. The young men rose and wrapped him up and carried him out and buried him.
>
> After an interval of about three hours his wife came in, not knowing what had happened. And Peter said to her, 'Tell me whether you sold the land for so much.' And she said, 'Yes, for so much.' But Peter

said to her, 'How is it that you have agreed together to test the Spirit of the Lord? Behold, the feet of those who have buried your husband are at the door, and they will carry you out.' Immediately she fell down at his feet and breathed her last. When the young men came in they found her dead, and they carried her out and buried her beside her husband. And great fear came upon the whole Church and upon all who heard of these things" (Acts 5:1-11).

This passage certainly is awe-inspiring since if we look at the above situation from a modern, pragmatic point of view, the couple's guilt is far from clear. After all, they brought to the Church their own money even though no one compelled them to do so. Why were they punished in such a terrible way?

This is a serious question that we need to answer so that we can be healed from the same illness that they suffered from since the current situation in our Church is very similar to the state of Ananias and Sapphira's souls.

Ananias and Sapphira came to the community where everything was held in common, where the Lord reigned. They did not come to give themselves, though, but rather to receive the blessing of such a community while at the same time remaining, in essence, like they were before, with their own self-interest.

In the same way, we bring to God a little bit of "ourselves," but the rest we consider exclusively ours and do not give God all of ourselves. We should act like we are all family here and we should make use of God's grace like close friends because God gives it to us completely selflessly, as a gift of love. God's grace cannot be bought and cannot be grasped as if it were our own. And when someone comes to steal that gift of love, craftily appropriating it for his own use, that is blasphemy against the Holy Spirit. It is the unforgivable lie, through which the entire substance of the Church is deformed.

Imagine how convenient it would be for someone self-interested, false, and hard of heart to live in a world of love! How easy it would be to subjugate a world in which everyone lives according to the laws of love and trust. And yet what a fearful thing it would be for such a person to enter that world!

This sin is a very dreadful one. The Apostle does not only cut Ananias off but he also testifies that the Holy Spirit has cast him out of the community because such a thing cannot be in the Church. Such a person should not even enter the Church because he will be spewed out by the Holy Spirit.

Everyone who comes to the Church always brings something essential for the life of the parish—their hands, their hearts, their minds, and their means. It was precisely thanks to these offerings that the Apostolic community was able to help widows and orphans, and everyone had enough of everything. This could almost be called a kind of Christian "communism" (except through free choice, rather than the compulsion that is the basis of Communism), since everything was "common" and everyone offered what they had and the Holy Spirit was the "distributor of grace." The deacons took what was brought to the Church and distributed gifts. This is how the part of Liturgy called the "Offering" (the "Proskomedia") came to be, when the deacons chose the best bread and wine to be used in the service.

Ancient liturgical monuments recorded that even the poor and orphans brought water to Church to be used for washing the hands and feet of strangers during Liturgy. No one came to Liturgy only to receive. Everyone came to give. They might have brought only water, but no one came empty-handed.

* * *

We can't buy anything from God. God doesn't sell. He gives. And God can only give when we have free hands in order to receive His gifts. We can't come to Him with hands full of bags for Him to fill.

Here it is key for us to understand the most important thing when we offer sacrifices. It used to be that people brought what they had but now that has taken the form of a monetary offering which can obscure our proper relationship with the Church. Many people think of the Church as some kind of a store—they come, pay a little money, buy a prosphora loaf, write a prayer list.... In the minds of those who are outside the Church or who have only just come to the Church, the idea of offering a sacrifice disappears because any true offering always involves effort. When bringing an offering, we must tear something out of our hearts. We must come to Church with a free desire to serve. We cannot just come and write a prayer list and then think, "Well, let the priest pray for those people." It must also be our prayer, our offering.

And an offering to God is a broken and contrite heart, nothing else. The Church does not need our material offering, and God does not want anything except our hearts. Do not turn the Church into a store!

Do not come to order something, buy it, and take it home. Proskomedia is the first step of the Liturgy, where we offer ourselves as a sacrifice.

7
THE PROSKOMEDIA

After the exclamation "Blessed is our God..." while the Hours are being read[1], the priest prepares everything that is needed for Divine Liturgy. Parishioners usually arrive later and are not there during the Proskomedia. That is how things are now in modern Church practice. However, if you would like to give the priest a commemoration list, it is best to give it before the start of Liturgy, while the Hours are being read. Of course, the priest can do commemorations all the way up to the Cherubic Hymn, but the proper time for commemorations is during the Hours.

The priest bows and kisses the holy vessels while reading the troparion for Holy Friday: "Thou hast redeemed us from the curse of the law ..." In this way, the beginning of the Proskomedia serves as the entrance into Christ's redeeming sacrifice, into the sufferings of our Lord Jesus Christ.

---

1 In the Russian practice, Liturgy is typically preceded by the Hours. In the Greek practice, it is preceded by Matins. Proskomedia can be done during either of these services, or even before any of the services start.

The priest proceeds to offer the sacrifice, because the main focus of the Eucharist is the offering of a sacrifice. We remember here the most dramatic sacrificial offering in the Old Testament, when Abraham in the land of Moria offers his only son as a sacrifice, the child of the promise. All of the prophecies of the Old Testament were bound up in Isaac. A new people was supposed to come from him. Abraham made his offering, but his offering was not that he killed his son for God but rather that he did not spare him, which was a foreshadowing of the Eucharistic sacrifice. We hear about this great sacrifice in the Gospel reading: "For God so loved the world, that He gave His only Son, that whoever believes in Him should not perish but have eternal life. For God did not send His Son into the world to condemn the world, but in order that the world might be saved through Him" (John 3:16-17).

Jesus Christ's redeeming sacrifice and the Eucharist which is celebrated in the Temple are very tightly connected to each other. It is one and the same sacrifice. We have gotten used to viewing the Eucharist and Communion as a commemoration of the Mystical Supper, which is not connected with what came afterward, but the Mystical Supper was really the beginning of the sacrifice of Golgotha, the beginning of the path to Gethsemane, and then toward Golgotha itself. They cannot be separated from each other. The Mystical Supper and the breaking of the bread is our Liturgy which is not something that we just observe like a play in a theater, but rather which we live. It is our entrance into eternity, into absolute reality, and we are both participants and witnesses of this great event.

But Proskomedia is a commemoration not only of the Savior's redeeming sacrifice but also of His incarnation and nativity because He was incarnate and born not in order to live but in order to die for our sins. For that reason, all the words and actions of the Proskomedia have a double meaning, depicting on the one hand the Nativity of Christ and on the other His sufferings and death.

On the Diskos there is an icon of the Nativity of Christ. We are used to seeing this feast as something happy, joyful, and almost childlike but in its essence it is deeply tragic. Everything that we encounter in Christ's Nativity we also encounter during Holy Week. The cave of Bethlehem and the tomb of the Lord are essentially the same thing. The swaddling clothes that the Babe is wrapped in are the burial shroud that Joseph and Nicodemus will one day wrap Him in. The myrrh that the wise men bring will be used to anoint His body after He descends from the Cross. The Diskos depicts both the cave of Bethlehem and the Tomb of the Lord.

When serving the Proskomedia, we are conscious of Christ's birth and incarnation in an unbroken connection with His death on the Cross because during the Proskomedia both His incarnation and His crucifixion take place together. The Proskomedia is a sacrifice that we participate in. And the priest (and it is a fearful thing even to talk about this!) is the one who offers the sacrifice.

He takes the main prosphora loaf that will be used for the Lamb, and with the Spear he cuts out a square piece with a stamp on it. The square piece—which is called "the *Lamb*"—he then puts on the Diskos. The Lamb bears witness to the Incarnation of our Lord Jesus Christ and to the fact that the Son of God has become the Son of Man.

The word "Lamb" is used in the Divine Services to designate the sacrifice. Throughout the whole history of the Old Testament, a lamb was always seen as the chief and most pure sacrifice, which was offered for the sins of the people. For the Jewish people, offering the sacrifice of a lamb meant "I have sinned. I have committed evil in this world. And now, an innocent, spotless lamb, the symbol of purity and meekness, defenseless and without malice, is suffering for my sin."

In the Holy Scriptures, the word "Lamb" is used to mean the Savior. When John the Baptist sees the incarnate Son of God at the Jordan, he points to Him and says, "Behold the Lamb of God, who takes away the sins of the world" (John 1:29). That is why this prosphora, which is destined to be used for the sacrifice, is called "the Lamb."

Then the priest, taking the Spear in his hand, cuts one edge of the prosphora with the words, "Like a sheep led to the slaughter ... like a blameless lamb before its shearers is dumb ... so He opened not His mouth." These prophecies point to Christ, to Him being led as a Victim to Golgotha. Then the priest cuts the bottom of the Lamb, removing it from the prosphora loaf with the words, "For His life is taken up from the Earth."

Next, the priest cuts the bottom of the Lamb with the words, "Sacrificed is the Lamb of God Who takes away the sin of the world for the life of the world and for its salvation." Having done this, he then takes the Spear and pierces the Lamb on the right side, on the part of the stamp that has the word "Jesus" while saying the words, "One of the soldiers pierced His side with a spear ..." He then pours wine mixed with water into the Chalice, adding the words, "and at once there came out blood and water. He who saw it has borne witness and his witness is true."

The Savior's earthly name, Jesus, is pierced with a Spear, because on the Cross Christ suffered in His humanity, with His divinity remaining passionless. The God-man Jesus Christ bore the sufferings on the Cross in His human nature, which is why it is the part of the Lamb with His earthly name—Jesus, symbolizing His human nature—that is pierced with the Spear. Afterward, the Lamb is placed on the center of the Diskos.

* * *

After the Lamb has been prepared for further use in the Divine Services, the priest takes out a particle from the second prosphora loaf to commemorate the Mother of God, saying, "The Queen stood at Thy right hand, clothed in a robe of gold, adorned in varied colors," and places the particle on the right side of the Lamb. These words are taken from the Psalms of David and are a prophecy of the Theotokos.

The third prosphora loaf is used to commemorate all the saints. The priest takes nine particles from this loaf, one after another, to commemorate (in order) John the Baptist, the prophets, the holy apostles, holy hierarchs, martyrs, monastics, holy unmercenary healers, righteous Joachim and Anna, and the patron saint of the temple, and the saints who are remembered on that day. The last particle is taken out to commemorate the saint whose Liturgy is being celebrated—either Basil the Great or John Chrysostom.

The commemoration of the saints during the Proskomedia is very important. We turn to all the saints for help, and all the saints stand with us during the services.

In a way, this part of the Proskomedia reminds us of the center row of icons on the iconostasis, showing the deesis, or supplication, of the saints. The Savior is in the center, surrounded by the Mother of God and all the saints, in communion with Him, praying for the Church. They have been numbered among the Heavenly Host and make up the Church in Heaven. The saints beseech the Lord, as the merciful judge, to have mercy on all of those standing in the temple.

It is not uncommon to call the Church still on Earth "the Church militant," since it is engaged in a constant spiritual battle. All of us are soldiers of Christ who have joined the battle for truth and love, the battle to maintain in ourselves the image and likeness of God. And the Church in Heaven, like we see during the Proskomedia, is the Church Triumphant, the Church that has conquered—NIKA. The Mother of God on the right side of the Lamb and all the saints on the left side are like a mighty, unconquerable army, surrounding Christ.

Afterward, the priest begins to pray for the Church on Earth. He takes a fourth prosphora loaf, used to pray for the living, and takes out a particle to remember Orthodox patriarchs, who stand before God in the Church like generals, who are the first in battle and who carry the heavy cross of responsibility for the Church. Then, he takes out particles to pray for the bishops and for all Orthodox Christians and also prays for his country.

Next, he takes another prosphora loaf that is used to remember the departed and takes out a particle to pray for those who founded the temple, all departed Orthodox patriarchs, and the departed parishioners of the temple he is serving in.

* * *

Finally, the priest reads the prayer lists that people have given to be commemorated. Often, we do not fully understand the reason why we make these lists. However, commemoration at Proskomedia is one of the greatest prayers that the Church has to offer. By writing these prayer lists, we are offering everyone up to Christ with a prayer for their salvation, healing, and conversion. When we pray, the Church fills up with those who are suffering just like at the Pool of Siloam. The Church has no more powerful prayer than the prayer of Liturgy, which can unite and fulfill all of our petitions.

All participate in Proskomedia liturgically—and I want to emphasize *liturgically*. Our offering does not just consist of writing a commemoration list and making a donation. Just like the Church liturgizes during the Proskomedia, so too do all of parishioners. They all take part in the liturgical act of Proskomedia by bringing their prayers to God.

A small particle is taken out of the loaf of prosphora each time the priest commemorates someone by name. There on the Diskos, close to Christ, the Lamb of God who takes away the sins of the world, close to the Mother of God, and to the whole Heavenly Church, the little mound of these particles gets bigger and bigger. The whole Church fits on the

Diskos, which symbolizes the whole universe, the whole world that God has created, with Christ at the center. Near Him, we see the Church Triumphant—the mother of God and the saints—and then also an uncountable multitude of particles, which represent the living and the dead, the good and the bad, the righteous and sinners, the healthy and the sick, those who are suffering and who have gotten lost, and even those who have fled far away from Christ, who have betrayed Him or forgotten Him, but for whom the Church is still praying and who God still cares about.

There are far more sinners than saints on the Diskos, which makes sense. We pray most of all for those who are in the most need of salvation, those who often, like lost children, are in a far country. We bring them to the Church in prayer like the four friends of the paralytic brought him and set him at the Savior's feet.

Now, all of them are within the same universal space, the same Church, in which the heavenly is inseparable from the earthly, which is why we say that the Church is "One." In the Church, the saints pray for the sinners and all of them together are around Christ, all alike will be washed by His Blood, and justified by the sacrifice of Golgotha. The Church is the great and astounding image of our unity with the Lord.

* * *

Proskomedia ends in expectation: The Lord lies in the Tomb. The priest censes the temple. Just like the wise men brought gold, frankincense, and myrrh, so incense accompanies this offering. The priest censes the star and puts it on the Diskos, covering it with a

Cross, the pledge of our salvation. Then, one by one, he censes the three covers and uses them to cover the holy vessels, like the infant Christ was covered by swaddling clothes and like the Savior was wrapped in a burial shroud.

Proskomedia is the great mystery of the seventh day, when the Lord rested from all His works, the blessed Sabbath after which we live in anticipation of the Resurrection of Christ, in anticipation of our salvation and the life of the age to come.

After the Sabbath has come to an end, we meet the risen Christ. This great miracle is reflected in the celebration of Pascha. Strictly speaking, in the Paschal service our liturgical triumph is realized in a kind of external way. The transition from Proskomedia to Liturgy is the fulfillment of the Sabbath, the seventh day, the end of the creation of the world that we now live in. As the priest censes the Altar, he reads the Paschal troparion, a hymn that serves the important role of making us realize the Paschal meaning of Liturgy as the mystery of the eighth day. The troparion emphasizes that Proskomedia and the beginning of Liturgy correspond to the end of our life on Earth and our entrance into the Kingdom of Heaven. For that reason, after censing the sacred vessels, the priest goes up to the Royal Doors and opens the curtain to mark the coming of the Lord and our salvation.

* * *

Liturgy begins with the priest and deacon praying and making bows before the Holy Table. The priest says the prayer "O Heavenly King ..." and then the angelic doxology, "Glory to God in the highest and on Earth peace and good will among men ..." because the service that he is about to undertake is an angelic one. An angelic function, so to speak, is given to man. The whole Church participates in Liturgy, once again manifesting its unity in a special way. Conscious of his human weakness, the priest prays, "O Lord, open my lips, and my mouth will show forth Thy praise."

The deacon approaches the priest and, asking for his blessing, says, "It is time for the Lord to act. Bless, Master!" In other words, everything that human beings could do has been done. Human gifts have been brought. Bread and wine sit on the prothesis table. Now the time has come when the Lord Himself will begin to work, when He will come into His own and will Himself begin His liturgical service.

With the beginning of Liturgy, we enter into the Lord's time, where there is neither past nor future, but only the present. Just like Christ at the Mystical Supper, before His Blood was poured out on Golgotha, already gave it to His disciples, so also when we take part in the Eucharist, we enter the Upper Room and are present at the one and only Mystical Supper. The Lord's time overcomes our earthly time.

When the prayers end, the priest stands before the Holy Table, which is covered with the folded antimension. He lifts the Gospel above the antimension and prays silently, asking forgiveness for his own unworthiness, and seeking God's help.

At this point, the deacon, standing in front of the Royal Doors, exclaims, "Bless, Master!" and the priest answers, "Blessed is the Kingdom of the Father, and the Son, and the Holy Spirit, now and ever and unto ages of ages!"

8
LITURGY AS THE MYSTERY OF THE KINGDOM

John the Baptist begins his preaching with a very important phrase: "Repent, for the Kingdom of God is at hand" (Matthew 3:2). The early Church lived out this eschatological sentiment wholeheartedly. When we pray the Lord's Prayer, we also proclaim the approach of the Kingdom of God, calling out with trembling, "Thy Kingdom come!" We are looking for the second coming of Christ, we long for it and are waiting for it. We are striving toward His second coming and preparing ourselves for it. The Holy Scriptures end in expectation of the Kingdom of Heaven, "'Surely I am coming soon.' Amen. Come, Lord Jesus!" (Rev. 22:20). However, at the same time, we have to remember: The Divine Liturgy itself is not only a manifestation of our expectation of the Kingdom of God but is itself the Kingdom of God coming in power.

As we begin the Liturgy, we bear witness to the fact that the Kingdom of Heaven has already arrived.

It has already come and appeared before us in all of its unfathomable majesty and we are now ready, with trembling, to enter into it. The Church that we are part of is taken out of this "temporal" time and the laws of our world now cease to function, just like the law of death which has reigned until now. The people who participate in Liturgy become victors over time and the corruption that comes from time. Heaven comes down to Earth and the Temple of God becomes Heaven on Earth.

Through prayer, again and again, we call for the coming of the Kingdom of God; first and foremost, so that it may always in a mystical way reign in us. It is not without reason that the Lord tells us all that "The Kingdom of God is not coming in ways that can be observed, nor will they say, 'Look, here it is!' or 'There!' for behold, the Kingdom of God is in the midst of you" (Luke 17:20-21). Christians come to Church bearing the dust of this world, but the unshakable laws of the Kingdom of Heaven always conquer all earthly institutions. Soon or later, we will have to leave everything earthly behind and come into the temple as completely different people who are ready to accept and inherit this Kingdom, partaking of the life of the age to come.

The Lord gave us the image of God's inexpressible Kingdom through parables. I would like first of all to direct your attention to one of His parables: the parable of those who were called to a wedding feast. This Gospel is read on one of the Sundays leading up to Christ's Nativity, when we commemorate the Holy Forefathers of Christ. God calls everyone to Himself without exception because, as He Himself says, "In my Father's house are many rooms. If it were not so, would I have told you that I go to prepare a place for you? And if I go and prepare a place for you, I will come again and will take you to Myself, that where I am you may be also. And you know the way to where I am going" (John 14:2-4).

The Lord wants us all to be saved and does not want any one of us to perish. "Come, you who are blessed by my Father," Jesus says, "inherit the Kingdom prepared for you from the foundation of the world" (Matthew 25:34). But at the same time that the Kingdom of Heaven is proclaimed, so also is the Last Judgment, since the Second Coming of Christ and the Last Judgment always go together.

Every time we go into the temple of God and raise our eyes to look at the iconostasis and see the middle row of icons, the row above the doors (the deesis row), depicting the Lord sitting on the throne of the Cherubim, we find ourselves immediately standing before the Supreme Judge. He is surrounded by His Mother, St. John the Baptist, the holy and all-praised apostles, and the whole Heavenly Church. They stand before Christ and implore Him that the Last Judgment might be for us a judgment of extreme mercy, a judgment where love conquers all things rather than a judgment where we receive what is just.

That is, in fact, what His judgment is. Through His mercy, each of us is given a wedding garment. If you take that garment, then you come to the wedding feast and abide in it, but if you do not take it, then you have judged yourself. "And this is the judgment: the Light has come into the world, and people loved the darkness rather than the Light" (John 3:19).

Liturgy begins with the words "Blessed is the Kingdom ..." These words fill us with joy because we are looking for the Kingdom of Heaven in anxious expectation. They also fill us with trembling because we are unworthy of God's Kingdom and often come without a wedding garment.

Every time we come, it is a test of our internal world: Do we have the Kingdom of Heaven inside us or not? Are we ready to approach Him or do we dread the Second Coming of Christ? Are we afraid of living to the time when we will become witnesses and participants of His Second Coming? Are we actually waiting in expectation of His Coming or is that just a familiar phrase, the meaning of which we lost a long time ago? Is the Coming of Christ truly a great feast for us, the fulfillment of all our hopes?

9
THE PETITIONS OF THE GREAT LITANY

We call the Divine Liturgy the "Mystery of the Kingdom" because our participation in it unites us to the Kingdom of God already here and now on the Earth.

All Orthodox services contain litanies. The first litany that we hear is called the "Great Litany" or the "Litany of Peace." In order for our souls to enter the Kingdom of Heaven, we must acquire the Spirit of Peace.

First of all, the deacon or the priest exclaims, "In peace let us pray to the Lord!" The words "in peace" here are a call for us to abide in spiritual peace. When we go to Liturgy, we should be at peace with God, with ourselves, and with our neighbors. It is not without reason that the Gospel teaches us that "if you are offering your gift at the Altar and there remember that your brother has something against you, leave your gift there before the Altar and go. First be reconciled to your brother, and then come and offer your gift" (Matthew 5:23-24).

If we are truly seeking the Kingdom of Heaven, we have to abide in peace. The Lord said, "Blessed are the peacemakers, for they shall be called sons of God" (Matthew 5:9).

In our contemporary speech, the word "peacemakers" does not mean quite the same thing that it meant in the time the Gospels were written. The Lord is not referring to people who try to reconcile opposing sides by making a lot of compromises. A "peacemaker," in the sense of the Gospels, is someone who is able to make and maintain peace in his own soul. This state of peace can only be obtained through great effort but it is an effort that builds us up spiritually.

St. Seraphim of Sarov said, "Acquire the Spirit of Peace and thousands around you will be saved." Those who abide in spiritual peace have conquered themselves and the devil since it is the devil who always tries to destroy this peace.

Acquiring the Spirit of peace is the goal of the Christian life. Abiding in peace is one of the highest states of grace that our soul can strive toward. True peacemaking consists of creating and building up this peace. The man who is able to keep and guard this peace creates peace around himself and brings that peace into the temple.

After the exclamation, "In peace let us pray to the Lord!" we start to pray for things that seem easy to understand but which, nevertheless, we need to try to comprehend fully. The Great Litany (or Litany of Peace) truly is great and its petitions are universal. It embraces both earthly and heavenly petitions, both the material and the spiritual.

"For the peace from above and for the salvation of our souls, let us pray to the Lord..."

We should never confuse the peace of our souls with mere comfort or convenience. We often find comfort by means of craftiness and hypocrisy. Dale Carnegie's communication theory has been very popular. He proposes all sorts of tricks that let a person convince himself of his own goodness and that he can create peaceful relationships with the people around him effortlessly. In reality, peace can only come to us from Heaven, which is why we pray for "the peace from above," which God Himself sends us.

After Christ's resurrection, the apostles gathered behind closed doors. Christ had risen but they had no peace in their souls. They came together just like they used to, only this time without Christ. The doors and windows were shut "for fear of the Jews." And then, behold, the risen Savior appeared to them and said, "Peace be to you" (John 20:19). He gives peace to their hearts which were filled with fear.

And these were the apostles—the disciples who knew Christ better than anyone else! How like them we are. Do we not know that Christ is risen? Do we not know that the Lord will never abandon us? Have the Gospels not told us and has the Church not preached to us about how God has manifested His power in the world? We know that the Lord is with us and yet "for fear" we close ourselves off behind steel doors and hide from each other and from ourselves. We have no peace in our souls.

Only God can give us this peace and we can either accept it or reject it, keep it or lose it, multiply it in ourselves or else waste it foolishly.

"For the peace of the whole world, for the good estate of the holy Churches of God, and for the unity of all..."

Do you see how often we hear the word "peace" in the Litany of Peace? A "peace" that we call into our hearts, that we call into the whole world, and into the soul of every person.

This petition has another important phrase "good estate," literally "the good standing." "Good standing" here means to stand in what is good, to stand in God's truth. The Church is an unshakable pillar that bears witness to God's truth. It does this not only through dogmas, Tradition, the writings of the Holy Fathers, or through proclaiming its ethical and moral teachings. The truth of God is proclaimed most of all through us. The world around us does not read the Holy Fathers, does not know the dogmas of the Church, and is almost completely unfamiliar with the Gospel. But that is the world that meets us.

The "good estate of the Holy Churches of God" is nothing less than each of us standing in that good, bearing witness to God's Truth to the world. And we can only bear witness to the fact that the Church is the pillar and foundation of the truth, that the Church is the keeper of the truth of the Holy Spirit, through our lives, through our communion with the Church. It is impossible for us to tell the world that while we ourselves are bad, there are other people among us who are good. The world simply will not understand us. You are the Church and the rest of the Church will be judged by your example. We pray for our "good standing" so that we may not be shaken, so that we may remain firm until the end.

And we also pray for the unity of all in love. Our Church is truly the catholic, or universal, Church; not only because its teachings are based on the Ecumenical Councils and not only because it is spread throughout the whole world, but first and foremost because it truly unites us all. Venerable Dorotheus, living in the sixth century, explained it this way. If you picture the world as a circle, then the Lord is in the very center and people are around the circumference. If you draw lines from the edge of the circle to the center and on each line draw points, that represents us on our path to God. As we draw closer to God, we draw closer to each other as well. This is an immutable spiritual law. This also expresses the importance of celebrating the Liturgy and the point of the existence of the Church, because the Church is meant to unite us all, gathered together at the feet of the Savior, "That they may all be one, just as You, Father, are in Me, and I in You, that they also may be in Us" (John 17:21).

"For this holy house and for those who enter it with faith, reverence, and the fear of God, let us pray to the Lord..."

This next petition contains two words which express inexhaustible spiritual ideas: "reverence" and "the fear of God."

In the Russian language, there is a word that means to fast or to prepare for communion—govet'. The word for being reverent is related—blagogovet'— or in other words, to "govet'" well. Do you see what meaning our fasting can have? For we do not have to just fast, but we can fast reverently; we can spend the fast in a state of high spiritual attention, a state of peace and belonging to the Kingdom of Heaven. That is reverence.

Now it is clear why we fast. We do not fast so that when the fast is over, we can immediately forget about everything and gladly immerse ourselves in all of the heavy things that the fast was saving us from. I prayed! And so now I do not have to pray. I fasted from certain food and so now I do not have to deny myself anything. I was doing something and so now I do not have to do it. Now I have the right to take a break from fasting. This often happens because many of us look at fasting as a burden. If our fasting was truly reverent, then fasting would enter into our very life and become an integral, indispensable part of it.

St. John Cassian writes that if fasting does not become a way of life, if at the end of a fast we go back to where we were when we started the fast, if we do not become changed people, then the fast was useless and unnecessary. If the fast did not change us at all, then we have only harmed ourselves.

Very often, reverence is born in a person through keeping a fast, which gives rise to some experience in the spiritual life. Abba Dorotheus maintains that practical experience is the most important thing in the spiritual life. We can be experienced in evil or we can be experienced in good. If we are able to cultivate in ourselves practical experience of good, then we will become virtuous. And what is virtue? Virtue is consistency in what is good. If a man has the virtue of mercy than he is merciful every second of his life. It is not a transitory state. A man who is kind is always kind and you cannot make him angry. If a man is chaste and pure, then he will not defile himself either by what he looks at or what he listens to. We are good only from time to time. We are only occasionally able to do good works. This is because we are inexperienced. And fasting gives rise to a little experience that makes us reverent.

"For our Patriarch (name), our Bishop (name), the honorable priesthood and the diaconate in Christ, for all the clergy and the people, let us pray to the Lord..."

The next prayer is for the leader of our Church community, for the one who, like a good shepherd, will stand before Christ on behalf of His rational sheep. It is very important that we understand what a great responsibility this is: to be an intercessor before the Lord for the whole people of God. In this way, Moses prayed as he led his people through the Egyptian desert, a people that was stiff-necked, disobedient, and unfaithful. They were a people that repeatedly betrayed God and Moses and rebelled, in spite of all the mercies that God showed them. At one point, Moses even began to call out to God, "Lord, did I give birth to this people? Is this people really mine? Why have I been given such a heavy load to carry?"

The Lord strengthened Moses and made him an intercessor for the people. At Moses's prayer, He remitted the sins of the people, sent them manna from Heaven, and turned a stone into honey. All because Moses carried the people in his heart like a mother carries her child.

This is the place of the bishop, the place of a patriarch toward his people. The patriarch can beg God to have mercy on us in spite of all our infirmity. He can even be audacious enough to ask God to punish someone or to forbid something. It was not in vain that the bishops said in the document "On the Social Doctrine of the Church" that the Church can even call on her people to disobey the government if the government is committing directly lawless acts. And so we pray for our hierarchy as intercessors for each of us and we also pray for the whole priesthood, the diaconate, and for all the clergy and the people.

"For the leader of our country, the civil authorities and the armed forces..."

The petition for the armed forces and for the people, of course, has to be modified over the course of time. But nevertheless, the Apostle Paul wrote, "There is no authority except from God, and those that exist have been instituted by God" (Romans 13:1). This often confuses people, especially when the authorities treat the Church with contempt and when the Church is desecrated. But we should remember that St. Paul said this to the Romans when the emperor was Nero, who many considered to be the Antichrist and at whose command Paul himself suffered. But in spite of the fact that the authorities were openly godless, the Apostle calls on us to pray for them. The people of Rus' did the same thing during the Tatar-Mongol invasion and remembered the Golden Horde in their prayers.

Then, we continue by praying for the whole world, which is in need of our intercessions:

"For this city, for every city and country, and for those who in faith live in them ... For those who travel by sea, land, and air ... For the sick, the suffering, for captives and their salvation .... For favorable weather, for an abundance of the fruits of the Earth, let us pray

to the Lord ..."

When we pray for "favorable weather," we are really praying for more than merely good weather. Rather, we are praying for harmony between mankind and nature, between mankind and God, and for the kind of harmony that puts nature at the service of man. The world was created in such a way that is comfortable and pleasant for mankind to live in. The world is not mankind's enemy; it is mankind's servant. When God gave this world to man to adorn and care for, all weather was favorable because nature was obedient to the laws of God's righteousness and love. Everything that was sent by nature was sent exclusively for the good of mankind. And so we should understand the words about "favorable weather" as a petition for the restoration of the true connections between mankind and nature: that nature, "the weather," would bring us good things.

When we bring our malice into the world, we destroy this primordial harmony, and nature is set against us. If we come into this world with love and live in harmony with God, then nature itself cooperates with us.

There are many touching stories in the lives of the saints. A lioness comes to a hermit's cell and drags him by the hem of his cassock to her den, because her cubs are hurt. And the hermit removes the splinters from the cubs' paws, treats them, rubs oil on their wounds, all because the lioness, a dumb beast, could feel the spiritual harmony in him. Animals know that man is their master.

Venerable Gerasimos of the Jordan raised a lion that led a donkey to a watering hole. When the saint reposed in the Lord, the lion laid on his grave and died. We could also call to mind the lion that dug a grave for St. Mary of Egypt at the request of the Elder Zosimas. St. Seraphim of Sarov tamed a lion so that it ate out of his hands. All of these stories bear witness not to some kind of supernatural gift but rather to the fact that a human spirit is in harmony with the Spirit of God.

In one of his homilies, Metropolitan Anthony cites the early Church Fathers who maintained that the Lord does not need our good works. He does not need our ascetic labors. He only needs there to be harmony between us and Him because in that case, we are incapable of being evil. The most important thing is to attain internal harmony—unity between man and God.

Liturgy is that spiritual expanse in which that unity is given to us.

"For our deliverance from all affliction, wrath, danger, and necessity, let us pray to the Lord. Help us, save us, have mercy on us, and keep us, O God, by Thy grace..."

Now we pray for ourselves since each of us has something that we need to ask from God. We can and we should ask Him to deliver us from every need and affliction and from the wrath that tears us up. If we ask Him something in simplicity of heart, the Lord will without fail respond.

"Calling to remembrance our all-holy, immaculate, most blessed and glorious Lady Theotokos and ever virgin Mary, with all the Saints, let us commend ourselves and each other, and all our life unto Christ

our God."

This petition unites us with the Heavenly Church. Together with the Theotokos, all the saints and with each other, we offer ourselves and all people to God. We give Him our whole life as a gift and an offering, as our Proskomedia.

10

THE ANTIPHONS

Immediately following the Great Litany, we sing the antiphons. According to established rules, there really should be two choirs, a left choir and a right one, and the singing should be antiphonal, that is the singing should alternate between the two choirs.

Antiphonal singing has been around for a long time, since the time of the ancient Greek tragedies. It first appears in Christian liturgical worship quite early. The Byzantine Church historian Socrates Scholasticus says that it was introduced into the Church of Antioch by St. Ignatius of Antioch (who died around 107). In the West, it was introduced into liturgical worship by St. Ambrose of Milan (c. 340-397). St. John Chrysostom (c. 347-407) introduced antiphonal singing into the Church of Constantinople.

The antiphons may have arisen from processions with the Cross. A procession with the Cross is the witness of the Church to the world. The people exit the temple proper and the whole space around the temple becomes an extension of it. The faithful carry icons and banners through the streets of the city and the whole world, whether it wants to or not, in some way becomes a participant in this act of devotion. Processions with the Cross are a witness to the power and fullness of the Church.

In the ancient Church there was a tradition. Sometimes, these processions would start at several different parishes and then all merge together to go toward a particular church that was celebrating its feast that day or in which there was some other important event taking place. During the procession, festal songs would be sung, praising the feast or the martyrs in whose honor the Liturgy would be. Once the procession arrived at the place where the festival was that day, they sang hymns by taking turns. Antiphons are processional hymns, hymns of gathering and preparation.

During daily services, the weekday antiphons are sung. At Sunday services, the services that you and I are most often present for, and on certain feast days, we sing the Resurrectional or festal antiphons. Festal antiphons are only sung on feasts of the Lord (for example, on Christmas or Transfiguration) and on the feast of the Presentation of the Lord, which is somewhere between a feast of the Lord and a feast of the Theotokos.

Antiphons prophetically depict the mercies of God which have been manifested to mankind through the incarnation of the Son of God. There are three Resurrectional antiphons: Psalm 102, Psalm 145, and the Beatitudes. They're separated by small litanies. During the antiphons, the priest stands in the Altar and reads the so-called "secret priestly prayers."

These prayers used to be read out loud. There's

no "secret" in them. It all has to do with how deep and grand they are. However, starting from the sixth century, they have been read quietly in the Altar which shows a certain kind of division between those who serve Liturgy at the Altar and those who serve it as the people of God. Many theologians think that this weakens the force of the sacred action that is taking place. Unfortunately, we are now reaping the fruits of this reduction because in the minds of many people, it is only the priest who serves Liturgy, only he who prays, and all the other people are only attending Liturgy. But this is false – all the prayers during the Divine Liturgy are offered up on behalf of all those who are gathered together. Each of us should know and understand the prayers. The antiphons and the litanies do not take the place of the priest's prayers but rather continue them.

The first antiphon is Psalm 102, "Bless the Lord, O my soul ..." While this is sung, the priest prays, "O Lord our God, whose might is beyond compare, whose glory is incomprehensible, whose mercy is infinite, and whose love toward mankind is ineffable: Do Thou Thyself, O Master, in Thy tender compassion look upon us and upon this holy house, and grant to us and those who pray with us Thy rich mercies and compassions."

Before the second antiphon, there is a small litany and the prayer, "O Lord, our God, save Thy people and bless Thine inheritance: preserve the fullness of Thy Church; sanctify those who love the beauty of Thy house: do Thou glorify them in recompense by Thy divine power; and forsake not us who put our trust in Thee." The priest prays that the "fullness of the Church" might be preserved that each person might possess the fullness of the Kingdom of Heaven.

The second antiphon consists of Psalm 145, "Praise the Lord, O my soul," and the hymn "Only-begotten Son and Word of God ..." which expresses the dogma of the Church about God in Trinity and about how the Son of God, who is consubstantial with the Father and the Holy Spirit, was incarnate, born, and took on Himself human nature. This hymn was composed by the Byzantine emperor Justinian I (483-565) who is numbered among the saints for his piety.

These psalms were not chosen at random. They contain deep, liturgical meaning. Unfortunately, usually only selected verses are sung which omit the very important lines, "The Lord in Heaven hath prepared His throne, and His Kingdom ruleth over all" which relate directly to what we are doing when we are standing there at Liturgy. The Kingdom, which is sanctifying our hearts and our life, rules over all. No one is unneeded in this Kingdom. Liturgy is an offering for the life of the whole world. It truly is the entrance of the Kingdom of Heaven in power, a Kingdom which rules over all and which each person can possess.

After the singing of the Second Antiphon, the Royal Doors are opened and the Third Antiphon is sung: the Beatitudes, the "commandments of blessedness." The prayer of the Third Antiphon goes like this: "O Thou who hast given us grace at this time with one accord to make our common supplications unto Thee; and dost promise that when two or three are gathered together in Thy Name Thou wilt grant their requests: Fulfill now, O Lord, the desires and petitions of Thy servants as may be most expedient for them, granting us in this world the knowledge of Thy truth, and in the world to come, life everlasting."

THE ANTIPHONS

Someone who reads the Psalter regularly will take easily to the Divine Services because practically speaking, Vespers, Matins, the all-night Vigil, and Liturgy are made up to a large extent of singing the psalms. Many of the hymns, even the stichera which are sung in honor of the saints, are largely built on the foundation of the Psalms. That is why it is essential to know the Psalter well.

* * *

During the third antiphon, the priest makes the Little Entrance which is also called the "Entrance with the Gospel." In ancient times, the parishioners would gather around the temple while it was still closed. The people would meet the bishop, and the Little Entrance was the entrance of the bishop into the Church. Nowadays, this entrance looks more like an exit, because the clergy leave the Altar through the north doors and then come back in through the central Royal Doors. In the ancient Church, the Gospel book was kept in a special place and right before this entrance it was taken out of its special place and so this procession with the Gospel book in the ancient Church was a particularly significant action.

Our Church has preserved this tradition in the way Liturgy is served with a bishop. When the bishop enters the temple, the Gospel is brought out to him for his blessing and then the bishop puts on his vestments during the singing of the antiphons and reads his entrance prayers since, as we know, it is the bishop who is the exclusive celebrant of the Divine Liturgy.

Now, the entrance with the Gospel symbolizes Christ going out to preach. The priest takes the Gospel book from the Altar table and lifts it over himself and exits the Altar through the north door while reading a prayer of blessing. He then enters through the Royal Doors. A candle is carried in front of him.

Liturgy is a concelebration between the Church on Earth and the Church in Heaven. In the prayer during the entrance, the priest asks the Lord to make the entrance of the clergy into the Altar also an entrance of angels who serve with them and who together glorify God's goodness.

It is very important that we know the structure of the Divine Liturgy, including the antiphons, in order for us to be able to participate fully. We stand and quietly sing along with the choir, aware of what is happening in the temple and the meaning of the words that are being said. This is our participation in the common liturgical prayer, in the very same prayer that the priest is reading in the Altar.

At the end of the singing of the antiphons, the deacon or priest raises the Gospel book and blesses the parishioners with it in the sign of the Cross and says, "Wisdom, stand upright!"

The word "wisdom" lets the worshipers know that the following singing and reading have deep meaning, and the words "stand upright" call on us to pay special attention and to be especially pious.

After singing "O come, let us worship and fall down before Christ. Save us, O Son of God ..." we sing Church hymns called troparia and kontakia. These short hymns tell us about the ascetic labors of the saint or the meaning of the feat that is being celebrated that day. While they're being sung, the priest prays in the Altar on behalf of all the faithful. He prays that the Lord would accept the Trisagion Hymn, which the

Seraphim sing, also from us who are humble and sinful and that He would forgive us all our transgressions and sanctify our minds, souls, and bodies.

11

THE TRISAGION HYMN

The Little Entrance ends with the singing of the Trisagion (or "Thrice holy") Hymn. We find the history of the origin of this hymn in the Holy Scriptures and in Holy Tradition. First of all, it is connected to the vision of the Prophet Isaiah to whom the Lord appeared as the Ancient of Days, in the form of an old man sitting on a high throne. "Above him stood the seraphim. Each had six wings: with two he covered his face, and with two he covered his feet, and with two he flew. And one called to another and said: "Holy, holy, holy is the Lord of hosts; the whole Earth is full of His glory!" (Isaiah 6:2-3) When Isaiah saw God, he cried out:

> "'Woe is me! For I am lost; for I am a man of unclean lips, and I dwell in the midst of a people of unclean lips; for my eyes have seen the King, the Lord of hosts!' Then one of the seraphim flew to me, having in his hand a burning coal

that he had taken with tongs from the Altar. And he touched my mouth and said: 'Behold, this has touched your lips; your guilt is taken away, and your sin atoned for'" (Isaiah 6:5-7).

There is also a pious tradition. A miracle took place in Constantinople that was witnessed by one young man who was taken up to Heaven during an earthquake. There, he was able to hear the angelic hymn, "Holy God, Holy Mighty, Holy Immortal ..." When he came to himself and told the bishop about all of this, the bishop decided to go around the walls of the city singing this Trisagion hymn, adding the words "Have mercy on us!" After this procession, the earthquake ceased and the city was saved. It is in this form that the Trisagion is included in the Divine Services. Such is Church tradition. In terms of documentary evidence, the hymn is first attested at the end of the first session of the Council of Chalcedon (451), when the fathers of the Church processed out of the temple singing the Trisagion.

It is worth mentioning that we do not always sing the Trisagion hymn at church. Sometimes other hymns are sung in its place. On certain feast days, "As many as have been baptized into Church have put on Christ" is sung instead. This is sung at Christmas, Theophany, Pascha, and Pentecost. In the ancient Church, these days were feasts that celebrated the birth in Christ of new members who had just been baptized after a long period of catechesis that for many of them lasted years.

In the prayer of the entrance, for the first time we are met with the idea that our liturgical service is equated with and raised to the level of the service of the angels: "Grant that with our entrance there may be an entrance of holy Angels serving with us and glorifying Thy goodness ..." the priest prays during the Little Entrance.

Over and over again, this idea is emphasized, that at this moment, the Church in Heaven and the Church on Earth are united together in a common service. It is especially clear during the Liturgy of the Presanctified Gifts, when we sing, "Now the Powers of Heaven serve with us invisibly ..."

The Lord accepts the praise that we sinners offer in the Trisagion Hymn that we sing to Him as if it were angelic praise because each person who has come to serve Liturgy is on the path to the Kingdom of Heaven. When we exclaimed "Blessed is the Kingdom," we proclaimed the Kingdom of Heaven, coming in power and now all the laws of the Kingdom are truly there present with us. We can praise God in the Kingdom of Heaven only like the angels, only together with them, only with the same words and the same voice.

We should not say that we are definitely saved and justified, like some Protestants do who consider themselves already saved. And yet, in a certain sense, it really is true because it depends on us either to accept or reject that salvation. Like was said to the young man in the Gospel, "Come, take up your cross, and follow Me" (Mark 10:21). We can either take the Lord up on His invitation or, like the young man, we can go away sorrowfully. The choice is ours. We can either follow Christ or act like spectators who take in everything that is happening around us as if it did not concern us.

The angelic praise begins, and we hymn the Trinity. Soon we will read the Gospel and very soon, He will appear. The Kingdom of God will come in power and it will ring out in the temple as the Word of God through Whom the world was created, Who truly became flesh and dwelt among us, full of grace and truth (cf. John 1). While the Church is waiting for the coming of the Word of the Gospel, that same word is being sung with the voice of the angels. That is why the Trisagion Hymn, that is sung as the Gospel is being brought into the temple, is so important. It once again sets in front of us the reality of the fact that we are present in the Kingdom of Heaven, that we must either accept or reject it, we must either follow Christ or not follow Him.

With our very own eyes, we see the same thing that they saw two thousand years ago. Christ comes and begins to teach. He proclaims His word, and many people gather around Him like in the synagogue of Capernaum, where He spoke about the bread that comes down from Heaven. Some hear Him, disbelieve, and leave Him. They do not accept the word because it has no place in them. Others say, "Lord, to whom shall we go? You have the words of eternal life, and we have believed, and have come to know, that You are the Christ, the Son of the Living God" (John 6:68-69). And they stay with Him, in spite of their unworthiness, how damaged they are, and how little they understand.

This takes place every time that Liturgy is served, when Christ stands before us and we wait for Him, singing the Trisagion Hymn, angelic praise which has been given to us to sing as true partakers of the Kingdom of Heaven.

12

THE EPISTLE READING

After the Trisagion Hymn is the reading of one of the Apostolic epistles, or as it is often called, the reading of the Apostle. This part of the Liturgy is also very ancient. During the early days of Christianity, when the community gathered to commemorate the Mystical Supper, the Good News, the Gospel, was proclaimed first. An Apostle would come and begin to prove, citing the Scriptures, that Jesus is the Christ. He would bring forth excerpts from the Old Testament about the Messiah and show that they were talking about Jesus in particular, Who was crucified and rose from the dead. That was the heart of the Apostolic good news.

Fragments of these sermons are recorded in the prokeimena which are chanted after the Trisagion hymn, right before the reading from Acts or one of the epistles of the holy apostles. A prokeimenon (from the Greek word προκείμενον which literally means "the thing lying in front") is a short hymn that is repeated several times and usually consists of two psalm verses, although there are prokeimena that are taken from the Gospels or an epistle. They contain the most obvious and most frequently encountered prophecies of the coming of Christ. They used to be read in full but over time they were condensed to two lines, one of which is usually the first line of a text and the other of which is taken from the middle of the text.

In the Catholic Eucharist, the Mass, the psalm before the Gospel reading is read in its entirety and is a true prokeimenon, a forerunner of the New Testament. In the Orthodox Church, the Old Testament prophecies are read completely at Vespers before great feasts. These readings are called paremia, or excerpts from the Old Testament, dedicated to the memory of the Most-holy Theotokos, to great feasts of the Lord, or the memory of the saints. These readings are selected according to the spirit and meaning of the event that is being celebrated.

We sing selections from the Psalms at Matins during the Magnification. The choir sings a line from a selected psalm, dedicated to the feast and then, as a refrain, sings the Magnification. All of this is an echo of the ancient Liturgy where the reading of the Holy Scriptures and especially the Old Testament occupied a prominent place.

After reading some texts from the Old Testament, the Apostle that was visiting the community would tell them about Christ Himself. He proclaimed the teaching of Christ that later became the Gospel (since at the beginning the Gospel was sacred Church Tradition and only a few decades later did the apostles record what had been their oral sermons). Each Apostle carried a Gospel that was either the fruit of his own experience of communion with Christ or that was the narrative that he had heard from those who had seen and heard Christ. As St. John the Theologian writes: "That which we have seen and heard we declare to you" (1 John 1:3).

The Church lives by the preaching of the apostles. When we read their epistles, that is the apostles themselves being present in the temple with us.

The apostles wrote to churches. The things that we call the apostolic epistles are really their letters, ordinary letters that they sent to those who were close to them from exile or while they were journeying. They are letters from a teacher who couldn't see them face to face. The community would read the letters like children, attentively and lovingly, and then would send them on to a neighboring Church, a neighboring community. That was how these letters became available to all Christians. And now, we read them and hear them. During the Liturgy, they precede the Gospel, coming between the prophecies of the Old Testament about Christ and the fulfillment of those prophecies in the New Testament.

The person who reads these epistles stands in the middle of the temple like an Apostle who has come to a community of Christians and is proclaiming to the people the salvation that the Lord has brought into the world while the deacon does the censing of the Altar, the reader, and then all the worshipers.

During the reading of the Epistle[1], the priest sits as the equal of the apostles, as the one who in himself marks the presence of apostolicity in the community, who continues the apostolic ministry,

---

1   In the Orthodox Church, the Epistle is often called the "Apostle" reading.

leading people to Christ and proclaiming to the people the righteousness of God. This is the essence of the reading of the Apostolic letters and then the reading of the Gospel.

After the Epistle has been read, the reader exclaims "Alleluia" which is Hebrew for "Praise the Lord!"

13
THE GOSPEL READING

The central place in the Liturgy of the Word is, of course, reserved for the Gospel itself. You could even say that this whole part of the Liturgy is dedicated to the Gospel and that everything that happens during it is preparation for the appearance and the reading of the Gospel.

The Liturgy of the Word, which is also called the Liturgy of the Catechumens, has a certain kind of independent life and internal completeness because for the catechumens, Liturgy ended with the reading of the Gospel after which they were supposed to leave the temple, according to the rules of the ancient Church.

The four Gospels that we now read were written in the period between AD 60 and about 110-115. In other words, for a few decades the only Gospel was Holy Tradition which the apostles passed on to their successors orally. And it was still truly the Gospel, truly the Word of God. Nevertheless, the Gospel as Holy Scripture appeared in the life of the Church rather early and was always taken very seriously.

On Pascha, we read "In the beginning was the Word and the Word was with God and the Word was God" (John 1:1). Often both in the Holy Scriptures and in the writings of the Holy Fathers, Jesus Christ, the Son of God, is called God's Word, the Divine Logos (from the Greek λόγος, "word"). As we open the first book of the Bible, Genesis, we see that its beginning is very similar to the first few lines from the Gospel of John, "In the beginning, God created the Heavens and the Earth. The Earth was without form and void, and darkness was over the face of the deep. And the Spirit of God was hovering over the face of the waters" (Gen. 1:1-2). God speaks His Word, and the whole world is created by that Word. The psalmist writes about this, saying, "By the Word of the Lord were the Heavens established, and all the might of them by the Spirit of His mouth" (Psalm 32:6).

The world, if I can say it this way, is "wordy." It truly receives its existence through the Word. The Word of God is so almighty and all-powerful that through the second hypostasis of the Holy Trinity, the whole world comes from non-existence into being.

The Apostle Paul defines the Word of God in this way: "For the Word of God is living and active, sharper than any two-edged sword, piercing to the division of soul and of spirit, of joints and of marrow, and discerning the thoughts and intentions of the heart" (Eph 4:12).

And the Word became flesh. The Lord appeared in the world and brought His word into it, imprinted in the Gospel. And that word is living and active.

The Gospel is more than just phrases arranged in verses, divided into chapters, carrying some kind of information. An ordinary text couldn't be so completely identified with its author, even if the text is an autobiography. Whatever a person makes, whether a book, something on a canvas, or music, cannot be the author himself, cannot be its own creator. But the Gospel has been left to us by the Lord as a miracle, God Himself abiding in Word. Certain elements of the Divine Services point to this. For example, when a bishop is serving, he takes off his omophorion and miter, which are signs of his high priesthood, signs that show that he is presiding at Liturgy like Christ presided at the Mystical Supper. The bishop steps aside because now the Lord Himself is present and He Himself is speaking.

During the All-night Vigil or during Matins, when the Gospel is brought out, we kiss it instead of the icon of the resurrection of Christ because it is the Word of God, incarnate and resurrected, the presence of Christ Himself at Liturgy. The Gospel is an icon, God's image. The priest censes the Gospel. We kiss the Gospel when the Lord forgives us our sins in Confession.

Sometimes it is said that if the Gospel as a book suddenly disappeared it would be possible to recreate it from the writings of the early Fathers of Christianity since they cite it so exactly and fully. And here's what's surprising—the Church spread during those times as the Good News of a Gospel that no one had read and maybe never even held in their hands!

In the ancient world, a book was a great treasure and not even the rich could afford to get something like that. For centuries Christians were only able to commune with the Word of God in Church, to learn it so that they could later live it, suffer for it, and incarnate it in their life.

The Gospel is the Church's banner, its spiritual treasure. When the Gospel was carried into the temple, it was seen as Christ Himself entering the Temple. And when the Gospel was proclaimed it was the culmination of the Liturgy of the Word. You can even say that it is a true communion with Christ Himself. The Word of God rings out, you take it in, are united with it, it pierces you like a double-edged sword, and it judges your thoughts and the intentions of your heart.

It is no surprise that in the lives of the saints there are stories like the one that happened with St. Anthony the Great. He came to Church and heard the Sunday Gospel reading about the rich young man and then went out of the Church, gave away all that he had, and went into the desert. Anthony was aware that what was read related to him directly and he joined himself to the word of God and changed his life completely, becoming a new man.

The grace-filled power of the Gospel that is proclaimed in Church is not in any way lesser than that of the live preaching of Christ that was proclaimed two thousand years ago in Galilee. It is the same Word that created the world. Through this Word, the dead have been raised, the blind have received their sight, the deaf have gained their hearing, the lame have begun to walk, and the lepers have been cleansed. Nothing has changed since that time because Christ is eternally the same and His word cannot lose its value or power over time.

The reason why we call the Church holy is that every moment of its existence, it is identical to itself. Everything that happens in the Church happens in the same way that it has always been. Christ teaches by His word and it depends only on us how we hear that word, how we take it in, how we live it.

Unfortunately, during Liturgy for some reason we are always waiting for the beginning of "the most important part," the Great Entrance, the Eucharist, Communion. Then we will really begin to pray! we think. But really, it all started a long time ago! When the priest exclaims, "Blessed is the Kingdom," that Kingdom is already coming!

For the catechumens, the reading of the Gospel is their main encounter with the word of God because all the rest is still inaccessible to them. They still haven't been born in Christ although the Word of God has already begun to transfigure them.

Even when this word was spoken by the lips of the Lord Himself, people reacted differently to it. Seven thousand people went into the desert having forgotten to bring food with themselves just to hear Jesus. The Lord spoke to them about the bread that comes down from Heaven but some of them expected Him to satisfy their needs of the moment and when they did not receive that, they left disappointed. "What strange words!" they said in confusion, "What is he talking about?" But the apostles stayed with the Lord because only He has the words of eternal life. And those words of eternal life are the Gospel.

The word of God at Liturgy is without doubt a true revelation of God. But we must know the Lord and hear Him. This is a necessary step that we have to go through in order to come to the communion of His Body and Blood.

The reading of the Gospel in Church is for us the possibility of encountering God. What is going on with us at that moment? How do we live that word later on? What are we like as we are leaving the temple afterward? Those are the most important questions that we need to find the right answers to.

14
THE LITANY OF FERVENT SUPPLICATION

After the reading of the Gospel, comes the Litany of Fervent Supplication. The Liturgy of the Catechumens comes to an end and a new stage of liturgical ascent begins. The Litany of Fervent Supplication is included in every service. Its petitions are similar to those of the Great Litany that usually begins each divine service.

At the beginning of the service, folded antimension lies on the Throne. Now, the priest unfolds it on three sides. Only the top part is left folded, which the priest opens a little bit later on, during the Litany for the Catechumens.

The Litany of Fervent Supplication is all-encompassing. It includes all the world's petitions, all of its needs and sorrows. However, even though the petitions are for universal, cosmic things, nevertheless the Church also prays for each of us.

When a Christian participates in Liturgy as its concelebrant that means that he has come to church not only to ask for something for himself personally but rather at that moment he has become the Church. That is why the Liturgy embraces not only the whole cosmos but also each person individually with all of his sorrows and burdens. To believe in the Holy Apostolic Church means to believe that the Church has brought all of your petitions, the whole depth of your sorrow and your joy, all of your worries and all of your thanksgiving to the Throne of God.

* * *

People who do not grasp the all-encompassing meaning of the Church often ask the priest to pray especially about some particular cause although the Liturgy itself contains the fulfillment of all our petitions. Serving *molebens* and *panikhidas* after Liturgy has become part of the practice of our Church. But if you're standing in church, the Lord sees you regardless of whether you've written a prayer list or not. Before you ask Him, He knows what you need and everything that you're going to ask Him for.

In my personal opinion, serving molebens after Liturgy does not make sense. This is a tragedy which has come about exclusively from the fact that a part of the people that come to the Church service participate in the Liturgy and a part of the people only come in expectation of "what is important"—when they hear their personal petitions and when the priest begins to pray for their health, success, and wellbeing, although all of those petitions are already included in the Liturgy. The Savior of the world brings His sacrifice on behalf of all and for all.

The question naturally arises: Why then do

molebens exist at all? Why do we serve panikhidas? They are present in the life of the Church as extra-liturgical acts. Neither in Greece or Bulgaria do they serve molebens after Liturgy and even in Russia this practice used to be unknown. Rather, a priest would be invited to someone's home or to some other place where he would serve a moleben for some concrete purpose, for example, for asking God to send rain.

However, if there is a need to pray for something special, for example, for a sick person, then the whole Church together should pray, not just the priest. There are special petitions for this that can be added to the Litany of Fervent Supplication—prayers for travel, for captives, for the suffering, for the sick, etc.

15
THE LITANY OF THE CATECHUMENS

Before the Revolution, there were no catechumens in Russia—there couldn't have been—but now they have reappeared in our Church. Once again there are people who need to be illumined, who need to be prepared for the Mystery of Holy Baptism, there are those that we need to preach the basics of Christianity to. These days, a huge number of people come to the font without catechesis. This should not be. It is absolutely essential that people be prepared for Baptism and that they have the prayers of the Church.

The catechumenate (from the Greek word κατήχησις, meaning "teaching, instruction") has been preserved in the Church for a very long time. All of those who wanted to be baptized went through catechesis. In the fourth through the sixth centuries, when the Roman Empire practically became a Christian empire, in spite of divisions and numerous heresies, it was an accepted practice for a person to be baptized as an already established adult. Children were rarely baptized. This tradition arose from a pious regard for the Mystery of Baptism and entrance into the Church. Additionally, Christians accepted pagans into their ranks only after serious preparation. However, when the Church was subject to persecution, there were no conditions for catechesis. Have you believed in the Lord? Do you believe in Christ with your heart? Life itself will test your faith ...

When the times of persecution had passed, the Church was filled with a significant number of new converts and grew a little impoverished in faith. In its own way, monasticism arose as a protest against this impoverishment of piety and catechesis took on a somewhat different form.

Catechetical schools began to be opened to help prepare people for baptism. The first of these schools were founded in Alexandria, and the first teachers were Clement of Alexandria (c. 150-215) and his pupil Origen (c. 185-254). The period of catechesis usually lasted between forty days and three years. Baptisms were far from an everyday occurrence. Usually they took place right before Pascha, on Holy Saturday, which was very significant symbolically. Baptism was seen as baptism into the death of Christ.

During the Mystery, the epistle of St. Paul to the Romans is read. "Do you not know that all of us who have been baptized into Christ Jesus were baptized into his death? We were buried therefore with him by baptism into death, in order that, just as Christ was raised from the dead by the glory of the Father, we too might walk in newness of life" (Romans 6:3-4). For all who were being baptized, the reality of their burial with Christ, the death of the old man, and their rising in newness of life was self-evident. Even up to the present day, at Nativity, Theophany, on Pascha, and on Pentecost instead of singing the Trisagion Hymn at church, we sing, "As many as have been baptized into Christ have put on Christ ..." This is done on the very same days that were set aside by Church tradition for the baptism of the catechumens.

St. Constantine the Great, the equal-to-the-Apostles, received baptism only on his deathbed. It seems paradoxical but even as he opened the First Ecumenical Council and headed a Christian empire, he still was not a Christian, but only a catechumen. For a long time, he was not able to be baptized because his conscience was burdened with many sins. Constantine fought, punished criminals, and spilled blood. He was not able to combine a life according to the Gospel with his duties as a ruler.

What happened with St. Ambrose was a curious circumstance. When it was time to select a new bishop for Mediolan (modern Milan), pious Christians chose Ambrose. He was raised in a Christian family, his grandmother was martyred for Christ, his sister was a nun who headed up a community of virgins, but he himself hadn't been baptized at forty years old. Only after he was selected as bishop, did he go through all the steps of the priesthood in four days: the first day he was baptized, the second day he was ordained a deacon, the third day a priest, and on the fourth day, still wearing his baptismal robe, he was consecrated a bishop because according to ancient tradition, new converts wore their white baptismal robes for nine days following baptism.

I'm not even going to talk about such notable ascetics such as Gregory the Theologian (329-389), whose father was a bishop, Basil the Great (c. 330-

379), and John Chrysostom (c. 347-407), who were all baptized after they were thirty. Baptism in those days was looked at almost like monastic tonsure—a new man was born who was to live a completely different life, rejecting the world and dedicating himself completely to Christ.

The true meaning of Baptism was much more obvious for the Christians of those days than for modern people. Later it became accepted to baptize only infants. Catechesis was then put in the hands of the sponsors, that is, the godparents, who, according to the Church, should raise the child a Christian and took on that responsibility before God. However, it turned out that godparents were not equal to the task so, as Nikolai Leskov noted rightly, "Rus was baptized but not enlightened."

Now we see all around us more than a few baptized people in whose minds the great Mystery of Baptism is seen as a merely formal act. Having been baptized and having received the possibility of salvation in the Church, they nevertheless have not turned to God, have not begun to live a spiritual, Churchly life.

Frequently, this kind of behavior is explained away as a tradition. Since we were born and grew up in an Orthodox country, since we were baptized at some point, then we should baptize our children, too. Maybe they will not get sick as often. That is a completely pagan approach that erodes the true meaning of baptism. Not only in Russia but in other Orthodox countries as well, baptism has become a beautiful but exclusively external ritual. People no longer feel their responsibility for the vows they have made to God.

The time has come to return to the ancient practice of catechesis. It is an extremely important period in a person's spiritual life. But what if when people find out what will be expected of them in the future, they get scared and change their minds? Many people these days want to be baptized but cannot even explain what God they have come to believe in and what has brought about their intention. Being baptized and joining the Church are, for them, two completely disconnected things. They look at baptism as some kind of a bargain that they're striking with God. I've been baptized and that means that now God will help me, but the Church does not have anything to do with it, God is in my soul!

If we are asked to be godparents, we should remember that it is a great responsibility! The invisible connection between godchildren and their sponsors lasts even into the next life. The Lord will without fail ask us where our godchildren are, why they are not in Church, why we did not do anything for them. Of course, godparents are obliged to pray for their godchildren but not only to pray but also to be a constant participant in the Church becoming part of their lives.

16

THE CHERUBIC HYMN

After the Litany of the Catechumens, the antimension is already opened and the temple is all ready for the offering of the bloodless sacrifice. The Church has already sent up prayers and commemorations, forgetting neither the living, nor the departed, nor the catechumens, and the deacon intones, "Depart, catechumens, depart ..." so that only the faithful remain in the temple for the Divine Liturgy.

Christians are called by the Eucharistic word "faithful." After the Litany of the Catechumens, there are two litanies for the faithful.

The priest reads the first prayer during the small Litany of the Faithful:

> "We give thanks unto Thee, O Lord God of the Powers, who hast accounted us worthy to stand even now before Thy holy Altar, and to fall down before Thy compassion for our sins and the errors of

the people. Accept our supplications, O God; make us worthy to offer unto Thee prayers and supplications, and unbloody sacrifices for all Thy people. And enable us, whom Thou hast placed in this Thy ministry, by the power of Thy Holy Spirit, blamelessly and without offense, in the pure witness of our conscience, to call upon Thee at all times and in every place: that hearing us, Thou mayest show mercy upon us according to the plenitude of Thy goodness."

This first prayer talks about people who are trying to stay faithful. If they are not trying to stay faithful then it would be difficult to call them "the faithful," in other words, Christians. After the next litany, the priest reads the second prayer of the faithful:

"Again and oftentimes we fall down before Thee and beseech Thee, O Good Lord who lovest mankind, that looking down upon our petition Thou wilt cleanse our souls and bodies from all defilement of flesh or spirit, and grant us to stand blameless and without condemnation before Thy Holy Altar. Grant also, O God, to those who pray with us growth in life and faith and spiritual understanding. Grant them always blamelessly to serve Thee with fear and love, and to partake without condemnation of Thy Holy Mysteries, and to be counted worthy of Thy

Heavenly Kingdom."

In this prayer the priest prays that all people who are in the temple at that moment might be able to receive Communion without condemnation of the Holy Mysteries. That means that all the parishioners should really prepare themselves to receive the Holy Mysteries or else it is unclear why this prayer is read.

Sometimes it happens that someone comes to the service but does not want to take Communion. Why? The only thing that can separate us from Communion, separate us from the limitless love of God is a deadly sin and nothing else. But more often it is laziness that is stopping us from Communion. We are too lazy to come to Vespers, too lazy to pray, too lazy to work on ourselves, and we do not feel like being reconciled to our neighbor and going to Confession.

Who are the prayers for the faithful read for? When we received Holy Baptism, each of us gave a vow of faith. A Christian is called faithful not only because he has entrusted his life to God but because he has promised to stay faithful to Him. It is for the sake of that faithfulness that the Lord gives us His Great Mysteries. Vows of faithfulness belong to eternity.

* * *

"We who mystically represent the Cherubim, and who sing to the Life-Giving Trinity the thrice-holy hymn, let us now lay aside all earthly cares that we may receive the King of all, escorted invisibly by the angelic hosts. What inscrutable words are sung at

Liturgy! Who can listen to them without trembling? Ponder it. We mysteriously represent the Cherubim. Is not like represented by like? And we represent the Cherubim ..." – Fr. Paul Florensky

"We who mystically represent the Cherubim ..." What do these strange words mean? We just know that while the Cherubic hymn is being sung, we should be still. But why? What for? I would very much like it if you asked yourselves that question often.

Coming to the Divine Service, almost no one understands the meaning of this festal troparion and many other words are not understood as well. This is by no means acceptable! It goes without saying that the Church has a mystical foundation, but nothing is secret, nothing is meant to be kept from those who are standing and praying on the other side of the doors of the iconostasis. The criticism against the Orthodox Church that we serve "in an incomprehensible language" is largely just. If we do not speak this "Orthodox language" then we should get rid of it, otherwise we are deceived and become like the Pharisees. The outer form is observed but at the same time, it is completely deprived of its spiritual content.

Why do we not change? Why do we not grow spiritually? For a very simple reason. We approach a lot of things only in a formal sort of way. We need to prepare ourselves for Liturgy, for the feast, so that we can sing the magnifications and troparion with the Choir, and all together say, "Receive the Body of Christ ..." say it with one mouth and one heart. We are not at the theater or at a concert! These songs are not sung to us. They're sung by us! We are all participants in this great and most Heavenly mystery.

Our lack of understanding of the most important moments of Liturgy is a tragedy. I would like to call on us all to pray with understanding, not to pray to God in words that we are not familiar with. We are speaking with the Father. We should not consider it some great work to seek clarification on what these words mean. And this is what they mean: You who are standing there in Church, who are mystically representing the Cherubim, who are singing the Triceholy Hymn, should lay aside all your earthly cares.

At that moment, each of us is given the opportunity to stand with the Cherubim and the Seraphim. They sing, "Holy, Holy, Holy," and we should join with them in one common, angelic doxology.

We are active participants in this mystery and not spectators. We are concelebrating with the angels and this is the culmination of the service, when it is time for us to lay aside all the cares and worries of life.

"That we may receive the King of all who comes invisibly born by the angelic hosts." This is an echo of the ancient or Byzantine world. In those days, victorious commanders were lifted by hand and carried through triumphal arches. That is how we should carry Christ.

* * *

During the singing of the Cherubic Hymn, the Great Entrance takes place. The King of Glory, Christ, goes to the Cross because the Great Entrance is the Savior's procession toward Golgotha. "King of kings and Lord of lords cometh forth to be sacrificed, and given as food to the faithful."

The deacon censes the Altar and the people gathered in the temple as he reads a penitential psalm, Psalm 50, which we can also read to ourselves at this moment. The Cherubic height that each of us is called to leads our souls to a state of deep consciousness of our own shortcomings.

It is no accident that right before the singing of the Cherubic Hymn, the priest opens the Royal Doors and stands before the Altar table and reads the only prayer in all of Liturgy that relates only to him alone and not to all the others who are present: "No one who is bound with the desires and pleasures of flesh is worthy to approach or draw nigh or to serve minister Thee, O King of glory: for to serve Thee is great and terrible thing even to the Heavenly Powers ..." This prayer is addressed to the Lord Jesus Christ Himself, the chief priest, before Whom stands an unworthy cleric who is entering the fearful realm of priestly service.

The priest asks for forgiveness from everyone serving in the Altar and from all the parishioners, censes the Gifts that are on the prothesis table, and as the Cherubic Hymn is being sung, he exits the Altar and goes to stand on the solea (the raised area in front of the iconostasis). He carries the Holy Gifts, the Chalice with wine that will become the Blood of Christ, and the Diskos with bread that will turn into the Body of Christ. During the Great Entrance, we commemorate the whole Church at the same time. Just like the Lord Almighty carries the whole world in His hands, the priest also when he goes out of the alter carries the Gifts as an image of the world, the Church, and the whole universe, for which Christ's sacrifice is offered.

The Great Entrance represents the Lord's entrance into Jerusalem—Jesus is going toward His suffering. This is the victory which the Lord attains through apparent defeat, it is how He takes on Himself through love and humility all the sins of the world so that the world might be saved. We mystically represent the Cherubim but at the same time we are those who crucify Christ. It is because of everything that Satan has put in our souls that the Lord needs to go to His death, and so the Great Entrance is for each of us a judgment, an examination of our life and our involvement in the sacrifice of the Savior.

* * *

The priest enters the Altar and places the Diskos and the Chalice on the Altar table, removes the covers from them, and reads the troparion of Great and Holy Friday, "The noble Joseph ..." the prayer about the Lord being taken down from the Cross, once again emphasizing the connection with Golgotha, the sacrificial nature of the Great Entrance. On the Altar table, the gifts are covered again by the aer. The gifts were on the prothesis table in remembrance of how Christ was swaddled as a babe. Now, they remind us of how He was wrapped in the burial cloth. As he finishes the censing, the priest prays, "Do good, O Lord, in Thy good pleasure unto Sion, and let the walls of Jerusalem be builded ..."

> "You who are like the Cherubim, do you not tremble before each other? You should tremble even more! Do you

know who is here? The King, Christ, Whom the angelic hosts serve invisibly. Don't you know that the Lord is here? He is with us, like He promised. Can't we now lay aside every earthly care? Can't we now forget about the crust of everyday life that hides our Guardian Angel from each of us? May that cover fall from before our eyes! May the wall that separates one heart from another collapse! Oh, what happiness for each of us to see the Cherubim in each other! Oh eternal joy! Let us now lay aside all earthly cares. All of them..." - Fr. Paul Florensky

17

THE SYMBOL OF FAITH
THE NICENE CREED

The Great Entrance is finished, the Royal Doors are closed, and the curtain is pulled shut. The church begins to prepare the faithful for the Mystery of the Eucharist by means of the Litany of Supplication: "For the precious Gifts now offered, let us pray to the Lord ..."

While this litany is going on, the priest quietly prays the prayer of the *prothesis*, asking God to accept this offering: "And make us worthy to find grace in Thy sight, that our sacrifice may be acceptable unto Thee; and that the good spirit of Thy grace may dwell upon us and upon these gifts here offered, and upon all Thy people."

* * *

The deacon intones, "Let us love one another, that with one mind we may confess ..." It used to be the case that after this exclamation, Christians would kiss each other as a sign of faith, love, and concord. This custom is still followed among the clergy. They kiss the Diskos, the potir (or Chalice, from the ancient Greek word ποτήρ which means "cup" or "Chalice"), the holy table, and then kiss each other with the words "Christ is in our midst!" and answer "He is and always shall be."

The deacon exclaims, "The doors, the doors, in wisdom let us attend!" In the ancient Church, the exclamation "The doors, the doors ..." was for the doorkeepers who stood by the doors of the temple and told them to watch the entrance carefully and not let in the catechumens or the penitents, in other words, those who were not supposed to be there when the Mystery of Holy Communion was being served.

* * *

When we sing the Symbol of Faith, we are not praying for anything, not repenting for our sins. We are making promises and vows.

The first time we sing the Symbol of Faith is when we receive Holy Baptism. After the priest asks us about our faith, we make our first vow to be faithful and then read the Symbol of Faith. Every morning as we wake up, we again vow to be faithful to God and to live that day as Orthodox Christians.

It is a vow that Liturgy itself imprints on us. We sing the Symbol of Faith together and confess our faith with one mouth so that we can then live by that faith, so that our faith can be known by its fruits, so that people can recognize us by our faith.

The Symbol of Faith reminds us once again that if we consider ourselves Orthodox then we should look at our Orthodoxy not as a *fait accompli* but exclusively as a path that we have chosen and now must walk. It is a possibility but far from a given.

Orthodoxy is not just a collection of like-minded people who are trying to assert their faith at the expense of others, people who always desire to be first. The only thing that the Lord will ask us is if we loved each other. This is the true criterion of Orthodoxy because God is Love, a love that is unreachable and unattainable by mankind but which in Christ has become reachable and attainable for us. We are given the ability to know God not through a scholastic knowledge of dogmatics, but through a real, living faith. And if we are given the ability to know God, that means that we are also given the ability to love each other.

The life of Christ is the life of the Church because He is the God-man and the Church is a divine-human body. "The Church is the body of love," the theologian and publicist A. C. Khomiakov said. A person who enters the Church and becomes a part of this body participates in this love in an unfathomable, mystical, supernatural way. The words "Let us love one another" are not only an exhortation but also a confession of our faith and the proclamation and appearance of that faith to the world. True love must be active. There is no theoretical love.

The point of Church unity is for there no longer to be anyone in the world who we are estranged from. Even within the church, surrounded by like-minded people, we generally do not love the people around us. We try to avoid people that we dislike. But St. John of San Francisco wrote, "The desire not to see a certain person is a lot like an order to have them shot."

How exactly are we picturing the Kingdom of God in these cases? Because in the Kingdom, there will not be a way to avoid seeing someone, to leave someone behind, to hide ourselves. But if here on Earth we consider to be estranged from us, how will we meet them in the Kingdom of Heaven? How can we look them in the eyes there if here they were estranged from us? We need to conquer this sense of estrangement in ourselves.

If we, calling ourselves Orthodox, do not love each other (and as a result, do not love God) then we are heretics. It is possible, it seems, to be a heretic while formally remaining in the bosom of the Orthodox Church.

At Liturgy, we exclaim, "Let us love one another so that with one mind we may confess Father, Son, and Holy Spirit, the Trinity one in essence and undivided," because loving each other and confessing the Holy Trinity is one and the same thing. If we have no love, then we do not confess the Holy Trinity. And the opposite is true—if we do not have true faith, then there cannot be true love either, although we are aware of examples of people who, while not being Orthodox, attained true Orthodoxy through the ascetic labor of faith and love. It is worth mentioning at least the Catholic Dr. Friedrich Joseph Haass (1780-1853), a Russian doctor of German descent, a philanthropist, who was known as the "holy doctor of Moscow," who used to repeat tirelessly, "Hurry to do good works!" or Alexei Trupp, a colonel in the Russian imperial army and the footman of the last Russian emperor, Nicholas II, a Latvian who, while remaining a Catholic, suffered together with the imperial family and sacrificially took on himself the full measure of their suffering, like a true Orthodox believer.

We are not Orthodox because we've been able to keep the dogmas of our holy faith unharmed. Rather, we are Orthodox because the Lord has given us, through true knowledge of God that hasn't been distorted through human folly, lies, or pride, the opportunity to perceive all the fullness of love. Dogmas are given to us with one goal in mind, that we might learn how to love.

18

THE EUCHARISTIC CANON

The second, even more important part of the Liturgy of the Faithful is when the Mystery itself takes place. The deacon's admonition, "Let us stand aright; let us stand with fear; let us attend, that we may offer the Holy Oblation in peace" moves us all into the most important Eucharistic prayer which is called the *Anaphora*. The ancient Greek word ἀναφορά in this case can be translated as "offering up."

The words "Let us stand aright; let us stand with fear; let us attend, that we may offer the Holy Oblation in peace" are not a prayer but an exhortation intoned by the deacon. The choir answers on behalf of all the faithful, "A mercy of peace. A sacrifice of praise." In other words, "let us offer up the bloodless Sacrifice (the Holy Eucharist) which is itself the great mercy of God that is given to us as a result of our reconciliation with the Lord and which consists in thankfully praising God." The priest, turning to the people, blesses them and says, "The grace of our Lord Jesus Christ and the love of God the Father, and the communion of the Holy Spirit be with you all." The choir, that is, all the people, answers, "And with your spirit."

Then the call resounds, "Let us lift up our hearts!" At this moment, our hearts should be striving to ascend up like fire ascends to the sky. We answer, "We lift them up unto the Lord"—in other words, our hearts are burning and turned toward God.

* * *

The Anaphora is the central and the most ancient part of the Christian liturgy. It is during the Anaphora that the bread and wine are turned or transformed into the Body and Blood of Christ. The Anaphora begins with the words, "Let us give thanks unto the Lord!" The choir sings, "It is meet and right to worship the Father, the Son, and the Holy Spirit, the Trinity one in essence and undivided." This is, in an abbreviated form, the content of the beginning of the Eucharistic prayer. The priest prays in the Altar, "It is meet and right to hymn Thee, to bless Thee, to praise Thee, to give thanks unto Thee, and to worship Thee in every place of Thy dominion."

Starting around the end of the sixth century, the prayers that the priest used to read aloud began to be done in a way that was imperceptible to the parishioners who were worshiping outside the Altar. The choir, as an icon of the people of God, began to sing only certain portions of the prayers.

One might get the impression that the priest is reading separate prayers that are separated by exclamations after which the choir sings certain hymns. However, really the Anaphora is one prayer that continues without stopping all the way up to the transformation of the Holy Mysteries.

Of course, the fact that the priest reads the prayer of the Anaphora quietly in the Altar impoverishes our understanding of the Eucharist. On the other hand, this change took place not at the whim of the hierarchy who were trying to separate the clergy from the people but rather most likely because spiritual life had already become impoverished and the people were simply not prepared for such spiritual exertion. By that point in time, there were already many people who were not communing at every Liturgy. Unlike during the first few centuries of Christianity, people no longer saw it as an urgent need. The priestly prayer is an attempt to unite everyone into one whole, but many people these days are not prepared to share that joy with everyone and so the meaning of having this prayer in common is lost. The prayer thus becomes a special priestly prayer and is transferred to the Altar where the clergy, standing around the Holy Table, always take Communion. The choir then sings certain pieces of the Eucharistic Canon, pieces that still join the people together into one united prayer and one united liturgical service.

The ideal is increasingly distant from real life. Over time, this becomes so ingrained that people no longer perceive that something higher is taking place—a united service, a united prayer, a united communion in the Holy Mysteries of Christ.

I do not know if it is possible to change the current state of things. It will happen only when the people again feel the need for a united communion, for the Liturgy to be served constantly, and for united prayer. Changes take place on the level of the consciousness of the whole Church and not through some kind of private acts and new interpolations, because everything in the Liturgy is living and meaningful.

The Church herself is renewed when a new sense of spiritual necessity arises among the Christian faithful. New possibilities are opened up, confessing Christ anew each time. If our Eucharistic life begins to fade, then the whole life of the Church becomes formalized, by the book, legalistic, and solely superficial. For the spiritual man is formed only by the Liturgy and not through any other means. The source of all asceticism, all theology, and all morality, just like the source of the whole life of the Church is the Divine Liturgy.

The level of people's spiritual life can be determined by how the Liturgy is served, and how they receive Communion. The way Liturgy is served reflects the life of the Church. In essence, the concepts of Church and Liturgy are identical. The Church is Liturgy and Liturgy embodies the Church.

* * *

"It is meet and right to hymn Thee, to bless Thee, to praise Thee, to give thanks unto Thee, and to worship Thee in every place of Thy dominion; for Thou art God ineffable, inconceivable, invisible, incomprehensible, ever existing and eternally the same, Thou and Thine only-begotten Son and Thy Holy Spirit..."

During the first part of the Anaphora, the priest confesses an *apophatic* theology (from the Greek word αποφατικός, or "negation"). Apophaticism is a way of doing theology that expresses the essence of divinity by means of denying, one by one, all possible limitations as incompatible with Him. It seeks to know God not by understanding what He is but rather by what He is not. And really we can only express our understanding of the Lord allegorically since God is so transcendent that human speech is incapable of accurately defining His Essence. Let's say for the sake of argument that you say that He is Light. That is clearly an insufficient description. You might say that He is incarnate Love and Mercy, but that also does not completely describe our conception of Him. It goes without saying that all of this is true but only to an infinitely small degree since we can only speak of our own conception of love, mercy, light, and goodness. And all of our conceptions will in any case remain insufficient, flawed, and unable to say almost anything about the Lord.

We can only say that He is unknown, unfathomable, incomprehensible, and unspeakable. We begin our thanksgiving with these precise words. Even the true meaning of the Name that He opens for us—I AM—tells us little because our life is imperfect and sooner or later ends in death. We have no truly independent life. Even when we repeat that "He is," we do not have the capacity to understand what that really means.

* * *

"Ever existing and eternally the same, Thou and Thine Only-begotten Son and Thy Holy Spirit. Thou it was who didst bring us from non-existence into being, and when we had fallen away didst raise us

up again..."

The resurrection of Christ is a new act of creating the world, a new creation. At first, the Lord created us, bringing us from non-existence into being. It would seem that the act of creating is one that is completely unfathomable because as humans we are incapable of understanding it. We do not even try to understand it, we only accept it as written.

But there is yet another mystery: Even though we already exist, the Lord creates us anew. Through His resurrection, He recreates the world, bringing it into being through His Church. What is old has already passed away, and the present has just begun. A new creation is being formed in Christ and through constant communion with God. We are participants in that new creation every minute.

* * *

"...and didst not cease to do all things until Thou hadst brought us back to Heaven, and hadst endowed us with Thy Kingdom which is to come..."

In this incredible prayer, we come face to face with the past, present, and future all flowing together into one, united time. In such a way, we begin to feel and speak as if we are already here on Earth in the Kingdom of Heaven. It is from this position that we give thanks to the Lord not only for creating us, not only for saving us, but also for having brought us up to Heaven and giving us His Kingdom.

We are invading Eternity which has already arrived. We talk about communion with God in the

Kingdom of Heaven because He has already given that to us. It has already been accomplished with and for us and we have only to stretch out our hands and receive what we are being given. The question is whether we really want it or not. Do we want to receive from Christ the salvation that He has already given? After all, the gift of eternal life is not an easy burden to carry. We have to receive it like a Cross. There is no other way.

The weight of salvation is measureless. A person might be bent under its weight. But each Eucharist calls on us to decide – are we really striving toward salvation or not? Do we truly want to carry this gift, the greatest of all burdens and yet simultaneously the greatest goodness? Or will we prefer to step aside? We can only enter the Kingdom of Heaven through the Church which the Lord founded, through His wounds, through His pierced side.

The Liturgy that you and I participate in is an unbroken chain of boldly touching the Body of Christ. Just like the Apostle Thomas, we "test" the Savior over and over again, placing our fingers in His wounds.

* * *

"For all these things we give thanks unto Thee, and to Thine Only-begotten Son and Thy Holy Spirit; for all things which we know, and which wet know not, and for all the benefits bestowed upon us, both manifest and unseen. And we give thanks unto Thee also for this ministry which Thou dost vouchsafe to receive at our hands, even though there stand beside Thee thousands of Archangels and ten thousands of Angels, the Cherubim and the Seraphim, six-winged, many-eyed, soaring aloft, borne on their wings."

We thank the Lord for this service, for accepting it as gift from us, who are unworthy, even though at this same moment He is being praised by the archangels and angels, the cherubim and seraphim, six-winged, many-eyes, soaring aloft, borne on their wings.. The faithful sing Him the same song that was once sung when He entered Jerusalem: "Hosanna in the highest, blessed is He who comes in the name of the Lord," and their triumphant song is joined with angelic praise.

The Lord is coming! And in the same way, we come to the Heavenly Jerusalem by receiving the Divine gift, by constantly striving to be with Christ: In His death and resurrection, in His ascension into Heaven, and in His sitting at the right hand of the Father. This is the main desire that should overflow in the heart of every Christian: "I want to be saved! I want to follow the path of salvation! I want to carry this undeserved, immeasurable, and unbearable gift on my shoulder because only then can I enter into communion with Christ!" Only then will this gift become the easy yoke and the light burden that the Lord spoke about.

* * *

Priest: Singing the Triumphal Hymn, shouting, proclaiming, and saying:
Choir: Holy, Holy, Holy, Lord of Sabbath; Heaven and Earth are full of Thy glory. Hosanna in the highest. Blessed is He that cometh in the name of the Lord. Hosanna to God in the highest.

The priest continues reading the Eucharistic prayer:

"With these blessed Powers we also, O Master who lovest mankind, cry aloud and say, Holy art Thou and all-holy, Thou and Thine Only-begotten Son, and Thy Holy Spirit. Holy art Thou and all-holy, and magnificent is Thy glory. Who hast so love Thy world as to give Thine only-begotten Son, that all who believe in Him should not perish, but have everlasting life; Who when He had come and had fulfilled all the dispensation for us, in the night in which He was betrayed—or rather, gave Himself up for the life of the world—took bread in His holy and pure and blameless hands; and when He had given thanks and blessed it, and hallowed it and broken it, He gave it to His holy Disciples and Apostles, saying..."

There is a prayer from the Liturgy of St. Basil the Great that uncovers the deep meaning of the Eucharistic sacrifice, what it is offered for and why Christ empties Himself.

When did the self-emptying or *kenosis* (from the Greek word κένωσις, meaning "emptying" or "exhausting") of the Son of God begin? The Lord already limited and emptied Himself when He said, "Let Us make man in Our image, after Our likeness" (Gen. 1:26). In the opinion of the Church Fathers, the creation of man was a foreshadowing of the incarnation of the Son of God and of His redemptive sacrifice on the Cross.

In that prayer from the Liturgy of St. Basil the Great, it talks about that self-emptying, about how "having made man from the dust of the Earth and honored him with Thy divine Image, Thou put him in a garden of delights ..." In other words, the sacrifice is already being brought. God is limiting Himself through the presence of His image and likeness on Earth, which have been endowed with immortality and free will. It is for the sake of man, that "image and likeness," that the great sacrifice is made. However, not only for his sake ...

"For when He was about to go to His voluntary, ever-memorable, and life-creating death, on the night when He was betrayed for the life of the world ..." The sacrifice is offered for the life of the world. Everything that God has created is encompassed by this sacrifice. But, in essence, this whole world was created for the sake of mankind. It exists inasmuch as man exists. It was originally arranged in such a way that we could live well and happily in it. The theologians affirm: the world is anthropomorphic, in other words, oriented toward man. However, when man sins, that same world is deformed, spoiled, and subjected to decay. The Kingdom of Heaven, the fulfilling of the fullness of time, when God will "be all in all" (1 Cor. 15:28), can only come through mankind.

✻ ✻ ✻

"Take, eat, this is my Body which is broken for you, for the remissions of sins."

This part of the Eucharistic prayer ends with the Words of Institution, which established the Mystery of the Eucharist itself and which have caused more than a few arguments.

During the Mystical Supper, the Lord turned ordinary bread and ordinary wine into His Body and His Blood by means of these words. That fact has led to the Western Church understanding them literally.

There was also a dispute in the Russian Church about when, strictly speaking, the change of substance occurs, when the Mystery of the transformation of the bread and wine takes place.

In our country, there was not much time for theology to develop. Because of the Mongol invasion and the fragmentation of the lands of Rus, there was practically no spiritual education. The only place that could provide a theological education was the western half of the Church, in the Kievan metropolia, which at first was under the rule of the princes of Lithuania and then of Poland. In 1631, an archimandrite, who would later become metropolitan, Peter Mogila, founded an institution of higher learning in Kiev "to teach the liberal arts in Greek, Slavonic, and Latin," a spiritual academy that was subject to Catholic influence.

Slavic young men were sent to study in the West in Roman Catholic schools. The training there was inherently of a scholastic character and our theology up to the present bears traces of this. At this time it happened like this: Orthodox Christians became Uniates in order to get an education and then, when they returned to their home country, they repented and again became Orthodox and in that way, brought learning back with them.

In the academy in Kiev, many subjects were taught in Latin and they carried out many translations of Catholic literature. There simply was not any other literature at that time and so the teachers strove to give the work a more or less Orthodox spirit. They borrowed from Protestants the means of criticizing Catholicism and refuted Catholic arguments by means of Protestant ones. As a result, many things were distorted and at the time people considered that to be

Orthodoxy ...

Since the most educated clergy served in the Kievan metropolia in particular, after the union of Russia and Ukraine and the formation of a unified Church under the omophorion of the Moscow Patriarchate in 1686, vacant episcopal thrones were filled by selecting educated people from there. One such bishop was St. Dimitry of Rostov (1651-1709).

In those days, disagreements arose about the transformation of the Holy Gifts, echoes of which haven't completely quieted down up to the present. Specifically about the words by which the Lord established the Mystical Supper, the Mystery of the Eucharist, when He took the cup at the Paschal meal and blessed the wine and bread and broke it, blessed it, and gave it to His disciples saying these words.

Catholics believe that these words in particular are the words of consecration that turn the bread and wine into the Body and Blood of Christ. This is the moment when they bless with Chalice and the Bread. In Catholic consciousness, the priest is an alter Christus, a substitute for Christ. The Eucharist is consecrated by his hands. But no one can take the place of Christ, nor is it necessary! He hasn't gone anywhere although He is with His Father and the Holy Spirit in the unity of the Holy Trinity in the Kingdom of Heaven. The Lord is with us until the end of the age.

The whole structure of the Orthodox Liturgy points to what is most important. In our understanding, the priest is not a "substitute for Christ" at Liturgy. He is the leader of the people of God and no more. That is why during Liturgy he does not accomplish anything by himself. The priest is the one who stands before God, beseeching Him to consecrate this Mystery.

When he says, "Take, eat ..." he is calling to mind how Christ said these words at the Mystical Supper.

Only after this does one of the most important liturgical acts take place. The culmination of the unbroken Eucharistic prayer is the epiclesis (from the Greek ἐπίκλησις, or "calling down").

The priest reads quietly, "Having in remembrance, therefore, this saving commandment and all those things which have come to pass for us; the Cross, the Graves, the third day Resurrection, the Ascension into Heaven, the sitting at the right hand, and Thy second and glorious coming ..." and then says out loud, "Thine own of Thine own, we offer unto Thee on behalf of all and for all."

After the words of institution, the priest prays, remembering these events as already having taken place in eternity. He even remembers the Second Coming since, as we have already said, Liturgy for us is being in eternity. It is gaining the Kingdom of Heaven. It is the life of the age to come which we partake in.

In us, categories are joined together that are incompatible, that do not fit together in human consciousness—the past, the present, and the future. We live either in the past or in the future, remembering or dreaming, while the present often passes us by. But the Kingdom of Heaven is the eternal present and it meets us during the Divine Liturgy. We are joined to the present and we ourselves become present because the Lord who is always in the Present gives us the ability to be joined to His Being through partaking in His Body and Blood. Even though we remain mortal and temporary, we nevertheless have come into contact with eternity.

We are already in a completely different world,

remembering how we were miraculously delivered from the danger of death. At Liturgy, we remember that saving Mystery, the Cross, the grave, the Resurrection, the sitting at the right hand and the Second Coming, as if we are already present in the Kingdom of Heaven.

* * *

Right after the elevation of the Holy Gifts, they are transformed. The Holy Spirit is called down to change the Gifts—bread and wine—and they are turned into the Body and Blood of Christ.

The priest takes the Holy Gifts in his hands and, lifting them up over the Altar table, exclaims, "Thine own of Thine own, we offer unto Thee on behalf of all and for all."

What exactly is the priest bringing that the words "Thine own of Thine own" refer to? These words refer to the Proskomedia. Recall how on the Diskos the Lamb is symbolically depicted with the Mother of God, the Church, the holy apostles, all the saints, all the living and the dead, all surrounding the Lord. The Diskos, as an image of the whole universe, as an image of the whole Church, is offered up to Christ. "We bring You what is Yours, from those who belong to You, on behalf of everyone and everything." Both Liturgy and Proskomedia are served not only in memory of the living and the dead, not only as a kind of prayer for our country, but also for the whole world, the whole universe, for everything that the Lord has made.

We have come and brought You everything that we could. Everything that we have belongs to God. We have brought You what is Yours. The bread is Yours.

The wine is Yours. I do not have anything that is mine. Everything is Yours and I am Yours ...

The Church's path of ascent to Christ is the way of the Cross. The priest crosses his arms as he elevates the Holy Gifts above the Altar table before the prayer of the epiclesis. This is the path of each of us and the path of all of us together—to offer ourselves and each other for others, from all and for all, to God. This is the path of ascent, the path of carrying our Cross, the only path to Christ, which leads to eternal life.

* * *

This moment is the beginning of the prayer of the epiclesis, the culmination of the prayer of the Anaphora, during which the Holy Spirit is called down to change the Gifts which have been set forth, the bread and wine, into the Body and Blood of Christ.

The choir sings, "We praise Thee, we bless Thee ..." and the priest reads the prayer that calls the Holy Spirit to the Gifts: "Again we offer unto Thee this rational and bloodless worship, and beseech Thee and pray Thee and supplicate Thee; send down Thy Holy Spirit upon us and upon These Gifts here spread forth ..."

This prayer is very short and not one that we can hear because the choir is singing during it but it is during this most important prayer that the Holy Gifts become the Body and Blood of Christ.

Pay close attention: we ask for the Holy Spirit to be sent on us and on the Gifts. We ask that we might all become the Body of Christ, we pray that all of us in the temple, the whole people of God, the holy Church, might become the Body of the Lord.

The grace-filled descent of the Holy Spirit cannot miss us. It is not only the bread and wine that were prepared earlier but all of us who are participating in the Liturgy at this moment who are the Eucharist. The grace of the Holy Spirit descends on each of us, turning us into the Body of Christ.

That is why every Orthodox Christian who participates in Liturgy needs to receive Communion of the Holy Mysteries of Christ. If not, all of the Liturgical prayers for us lose their meaning. Judge for yourselves: We stand there during the Eucharistic Canon, we all pray that the Holy Spirit might descend on us, the Lord sends Him to us, and then we refuse to receive Him! We find ourselves in a contradictory position. First we pray for the Gifts and then we turn away from them.

* * *

The meaning of the epiclesis is emphasized by a special prayer that was originally neither part of the Liturgy of St. Basil the Great nor the Liturgy of St. John Chrysostom, but was a later addition. I'm referring to the troparion of the Third Hour about the calling down of the Holy Spirit: "O Lord Who at the third hour did send down Thine All-holy Spirit upon Thine apostles, take Him not from us, O Good One, but renew Him in us who pray to Thee."

This troparion is not part of the Eucharist prayer. It was added as one more affirmation that the changing of the Holy Gifts occurs not at the moment when Christ's words are recited but at the moment when the Holy Spirit is invoked. The Holy Spirit accomplishes this Mystery and He changes the bread and wine into the Body and Blood of Christ.

The priest raises his hands and reads three times, "Create in me a clean heart, O God, and renew a right spirit within me. Cast me not away from Thy presence and take not Thy Holy Spirit away from me."

Unfortunately, the troparion interrupts the priestly prayer because in many Local Churches[1] it is read before the prayer of the epiclesis.

Afterward, the deacon, pointing at the Holy Gifts, entreats, "Bless, Master, the holy bread." The priest, continuing the prayer of the epiclesis, points to the Lamb and says, "Make this bread the precious Body of Thy Christ. Amen." The deacon answers, "Amen!" on behalf of the entire Church.

Then, the deacon points to the Chalice with the words, "Bless, Master, the holy cup." The priest adds, "And that which is in this cup the precious Blood of Thy Christ." The deacon and all the people with him answer, "Amen!"

The deacon then points first at the Diskos and then at the Chalice and says, "Bless them both, Master." The priest, blessing the bread and wine, says, "Changing them by Thy Holy Spirit." The deacon and the priest make three bows before the holy table and say "Amen" three times.

* * *

The Eucharistic prayer is offered up to God the

---

[1] Translator: In Orthodox ecclesiology, the universal Church is made up of what are known as "Local Churches" that cover different geographical areas. For example, the Church of Constantinople, the Church of Alexandria, the Church of Antioch, the Church of Jerusalem, the Church of Russia, etc.

Father. It is precisely to Him that the Church turns, and the Church is the Body of Christ. As St. Justin Popovich said, "The Church is our Lord Jesus Christ." It is a divine-human organism and if the God-man turns toward God then He turns to Him as to His Father. When we pray "Send down Thy Holy Spirit ..." we are speaking to God the Father and it is at this point that the change into the Flesh and Blood of Christ takes place, as a sort of new creation of the world.

At this point, the priest can only stand back. He blesses the action, but the Mystery is accomplished because the Lord hears His Church. We call out, "Make this bread the precious Body of Thy Christ ... changing them by Thy Holy Spirit" because God is sending His Spirit so that the bread and wine may become the Body and Blood of Christ.

This the culmination of the whole Eucharistic prayer and yet, very unfortunately, many of us hardly notice it because hardly anyone knows what's happening in the Altar at this point. This prayer is done quietly in the Orthodox Church while in the Catholic Church it is read aloud. It is very sad that the people at Liturgy, at the most majestic moment, do not participate with their hearts and their prayers. The whole Church should loudly repeat the "Amen, amen, amen!" when the deacon exclaims it on behalf of the whole church. That "amen" is our acceptance of what God is doing. It is our joint work with God, which in Greek is called "Liturgy."

* * *

Immediately after the prayer of the epiclesis, the priest prays, "That to those who shall partake thereof they may be unto cleansing of soul, unto remission of sins, unto the communion of Thy Holy Spirit, unto the fulfillment of the Kingdom of Heaven, unto boldness toward Thee, and not unto judgment or unto condemnation."

This prayer is especially profound in the Liturgy of St. Basil the Great: "As for us, partakers of the one Bread and one Cup, unite us all to one another in communion of the one Holy Spirit ..."

The priest intercedes with God on behalf of the living and the dead, "And again we offer unto Thee this rational worship for those who in the faith have gone before us to their rest; patriarchs, prophets, apostles, preachers, evangelists, martyrs, confessors, ascetics, and every righteous spirit who has completed this life in faith."

The prayer that begins with the words "It is truly meet..." ends with the Church interceding for the whole world, which includes all of its needs and all the people who live in it. It is the Church's prayer before the Body and Blood of Christ, a cosmic prayer that embraces the whole universe. Just like Christ was crucified for the life of the whole world, the Church also serves the Eucharist on behalf of the whole world.

At this point, we are participating in the most important liturgical commemoration. It is like a second Proskomedia. Remember that during the Proskomedia, the priest stood before the Lamb and remembered all the saints and then all the living and the departed. That same prayer is now repeated but this time before the true Flesh and Blood of Christ. The priest prays for the universe, for the whole cosmos, and it is like we are again making commemorations at the Proskomedia. The Liturgy brings us back to the beginning of our offering because we are again commemorating the whole Church, but this time a Church that has already been established as the Body of Christ.

19
PREPARATION FOR COMMUNION
THE LORD'S PRAYER

As the Eucharistic prayer ends, we move into the part of Liturgy of the Faithful where the Church prepares the faithful to receive Holy Communion and then the clergy and faithful commune.

The Litany before the Lord's Prayer comes next, "Having remembered all the saints, again and again in peace let us pray to the Lord ..." which is accompanied by special petitions. It spiritually prepares each participant in Liturgy to receive communion of the Holy Mysteries of Christ and in it, we pray that God would accept our sacrifice, give us the grace of the Holy Spirit and let us receive the Gift without condemnation.

The priest prays, "Unto Thee we commend our whole life and our hope, O Master who lovest mankind; and we beseech Thee, and pray Thee, and supplicate Thee: make us worthy to partake of the Heavenly and terrible Mysteries of this sacred and spiritual table, with a pure conscience; unto remission of sins, unto forgiveness of transgressions, unto communion of Thy Holy Spirit, unto inheritance of the Kingdom of Heaven, unto boldness toward Thee, and not unto judgment nor unto condemnation."

Afterward, the priest asks that we be vouchsafed "with boldness and without condemnation to call upon" our Heavenly Father.

* * *

The "Our Father" rings out like a Eucharistic prayer. We request our daily bread which during the Eucharist has become the Body of Christ. The parishioners who have gathered for Liturgy are humanity, called to become the son of God.

Jesus gave the "Our Father" to the apostles in response to their request that He teach them to pray. Why are there so many other prayers? If you pay close attention, all of them are in some way or another a rephrasing of the Lord's Prayer. Every prayer from the Holy Fathers is an interpretation of this prayer. In reality, we always offer God the same prayer but it just changes in our prayer rule according to our different life circumstances.

The three things that make up prayer are repentance, thanksgiving, and petitions. The "Our Father" is in this sense something a little different. It goes without saying that it does contain petitions but petitions of a particular kind—petitions for what we usually forget to ask for. The "Our Father" is a signpost, pointing out the path to God and a request for help on that path. The Lord's Prayer encapsulates the whole Christian world. Everything converges in this prayer, the whole meaning of our Christian life, our life in God, is opened.

The prayer begins with two simple and seemingly easy to understand words: "Our Father ..." We are used to thinking of ourselves as God's children. But it is one thing to know that God calls Himself our Father and it is something else entirely to live up to that relationship. Generally speaking, only the Son, the second Person of the Holy Trinity, can call God His Father. And so, when Jesus teaches His apostles this prayer, humanity is exalted beyond measure. God places man next to Himself and exalts him to an unimaginable level. We and the Son of God both turn to God the Father with the very same words. It is difficult for us even to comprehend this ...

The prodigal son, turning to his father, wants to be received as a hired servant but the father does not even let him finish speaking. The Lord does not need slaves or hired servants. Only sons can truly be close to Him. When we ask God for something, we often turn to Him as if we were strangers, either like subordinates talking to their boss, like beggars talking to a rich man who might give them something out of his generosity, or else like we are talking to a great unknown and unexplored source of grace, healing and miracles, but that is impersonal, unknowable, and with which we are completely unfamiliar. Our soul feels like God is so distant, so unknowable, and so great that it is unthinkable to talk to Him in such familiar terms like we see in the prayers. It only becomes possible if He is truly close to us. Unfortunately, we do not always thirst for that sonship, we do not always yearn for Him and sometimes, we even fear Him. We feel much more comfortable relating to God like some detached, all-powerful Being, unknowable and inexpressible. But if

He is our Father then that means that we have been given the ability to know Him. Otherwise, the prayer loses its meaning.

Seek and ye shall find. But our search for the knowledge of God should be a constant yearning and not just something that pops up from time to time. We can only know God through Christ, only through His Holy Church, only through the Mysteries, only by means of spiritual struggle. That is how the Son of God redeems mankind and makes us partakers of Divinity through the crucifixion, the death on the Cross, and the Resurrection.

The truth is, this sonship is in each of us as the image and likeness of God. We do not need to look for it somewhere outside ourselves, in some books or textbooks. At the same time, we need to keep in mind that if God, Who is Love, is our Father then we should be each other's neighbors, we should welcome one another. Alone, without each other, we will not be the children of God.

In the beginning, the Lord created humanity as a Church. "It is not good for man to be alone." He said, "Let Us make man a helper like unto him" (Gen 2:6). By creating Eve from Adam's rib, the Lord is not only revealing an image of marriage but first and foremost, an image of the Church. A part of Adam is taken out and he becomes incomplete, but then Eve is also incomplete without Adam. There should only be one flesh and that one body in Christ is the Church. Humanity cannot be complete until people are united to each other in Christ, until they replenish each other. The commandment "Love your neighbor as yourself" (Matt. 22:39) calls on humanity to abide in love. We cannot experience the fullness of existence while we are still closed off in ourselves, poisoned by self-love and egoism. We destroy ourselves and deny fullness both to ourselves and others. The fullness that is contained in the word "our" allows us to be the Church and to be saved together.

"Who art in Heaven..."

God's commandments constantly emphasize: The Lord has nothing in common with anything material. It was said, "You shall not make for yourself a graven image or a depiction of what is in the Heaven above or on the Earth below or in the water under the Earth. Do not bow down and serve them for I am the Lord your God" (Exod. 20:4-5). Why does the prayer mention Heaven? We know that God is not only everywhere present but also that He fills all things. It is no accident that the word "Almighty" in Russian means "holder of all things." The ancient Jews saw God first and foremost as the father of the Jews, God's chosen people. This is also typical for those who confess their faith as the true and Orthodox faith. But when we say "Who art in Heaven," we confess that God's fatherhood is all-encompassing.

Our confession lies precisely in the fact that we acknowledge God to be the Father of all people since He abides in the Heavens. Of course, when we talk about the Heavens, we do not mean certain layers of the atmosphere, the airless expanses of space and clusters of stars, but rather the spiritual world, the world that is unseen and all-encompassing. God's fatherhood covers all of His creation. There is nothing in this world that is not covered by His divine love.

Every creature that the Lord has made, every

person is a child of God, and not just us the "chosen people," and "royal priesthood," as we Orthodox Christians have gotten used to thinking of ourselves. The ancient Christian teacher Tertullian (c. 155/165 – 220/240) said, "The soul is, according to its nature, Christian." That means that all people, no matter what part of the globe they're born in, what culture or century they're born into, are born first and foremost in order to become Christians and learn to see in God their Father. For the Lord, there is no one who is foreign or removed from his fatherhood. Each of us should keep that in mind because that is God's providence for the world.

"Hallowed be Thy name…"

When the Lord revealed His name to Moses, He said, "I am" (Exod. 3:14). In other words, "I am the One Who exists." That means that only God Himself is truly real and everything else has a relative existence, existing only in as much as He exists. God cannot be completely defined and described. His name, which contains His Essence, is also unknowable, even the one that He found it possible to reveal to mankind, Yahweh or Jehovah.

The Old Testament Jews were forbidden to speak the name of God. Only once a year, during the offering of the Passover sacrifice, while the priest was sprinkling the Holy of Holies with blood, he said the name aloud. The rest of the time, words like "the Lord," "the Almighty," or "Sabaoth," were used instead, which expressed certain of God's characteristics but by no means His Essence. There are many terms of that sort but we will never be able to know God's true name. It is incomprehensible to us and so we only ask that it may be hallowed.

However, while praying at the Mystical Supper, Jesus says, "I have manifested Your name to the people" (John 17:6). What is this name that Christ has revealed to people? He revealed Himself to us because as He Himself said, "All Mine are Yours, and Yours are Mine" (John 17:10).

To know the name of God is to know God Himself and the name that the Lord has revealed to mankind gives us that ability. God is known through His Son. But the knowledge of God is not hidden in all the theological definitions that we use, nor in us comprehending certain deep truths. True knowledge of God is found in union with Him.

Our first union with God is given to us by the Lord through Holy Baptism, during which the Prayer for the Naming of a Child is read, including: "that Thy Holy Name may remain unrejected" by the child. God's name is placed on us, and no other. Christ is not afraid to trust us with His name. He is not worried that we will use it for harm. Only after that is the child given the name of some saint or other, but that name is only a supplement to the Divine name, the name "Christian."

We pray "hallowed be Thy name ..." but in what way can we glorify the name of God? We do not glorify His name by shouting it on every corner. We do not make it so that everyone might see the light coming from Him by writing His name in large letters in graffiti. Rather, we pray that for as long as we bear His name, people might see in us true Christians, that His name might be hallowed in us. Picture a man walking along the street. He starts to talk with someone and right away everyone can see that it is a Christian standing before them. All of his actions are a manifestation and confirmation of His divine name, because the name of God is hallowed through us.

"Thy Kingdom come..."

We pray for the Second Coming of Christ, the Last Judgment, the victory over evil, and the defeat of the Antichrist. We call on the Lord to come to us because we are faithful to Him and ready to meet Him. The Eucharistic prayer of the early Christians sounded like, "may the form of this world pass away." In other words, "grant, O Lord, that this world might soon come to an end and that Your Kingdom might arrive." They prayed for this even though they knew perfectly well that in order for their hopes to be realized, it would unavoidably entail the coming of the Antichrist and persecutions against Christians but that did not make them afraid. On the contrary, they longed for it so that every evil that disfigures the world might quickly disappear and so that the righteousness of God might reign within every human person.

"Thy will be done on Earth as it is in Heaven..."

It is God's providence for mankind to lead us all to salvation. However, that striving must define our whole life. I'm speaking about our readiness to entrust ourselves into the hands of God, about the capacity that each of us has to be like Christ, who in the garden of Gethsemane called out, "My Father, if this cannot pass unless I drink it, Your will be done" (Matt. 26:42).

It takes no great effort to entrust ourselves to

God when we feel confident in our own strength, but to trust Him like the Apostle Peter did when he walked to Christ on the stormy waters, to trust ourselves to Him in the moment when all around we see impenetrable darkness and when we have almost lost all hope of salvation ... that requires asceticism.

While praying for His disciples, Christ says to the Father, "All Mine are Yours, and Yours are Mine" (John 17:10), thereby emphasizing that the will of God the Son and of God the Father is united. In the same way, the manifestation of our free will should be in line with the will of God, placed in us from the beginning, since we are created in His image and likeness. Commending ourselves into the hands of God, giving ourselves over to His will, we pray that the Lord's gifts may be manifested in us in their fullness. Only when we have entrusted ourselves completely to God and have said to Him from our whole hearts, "All that is mine is Yours," will we hear His answer: "All that is Mine is yours."

God's will for each of us also defines our paths to salvation. These paths can turn out to be winding and not at all obvious to us ourselves. For some of us, it might seem like the will of God is hidden, like in fairy tales, across seven seas and sealed with seven seals. Many go from elder to elder, in search of some kind of especially "enlightened" or experienced priests.

Unfortunately, for many people, looking for the will of God amounts almost to fortune-telling. Is it His will for me to buy a new apartment? Or for me to go to college? Should I change jobs? Get married now or take my time with it? Frequently, we confuse spiritual seeking with day to day comfort. For true believers, this looks more than strange. After all, God has given us our reason and life experience to resolve those kinds of uncertainties. If we begin our search for the will of God on such a primitive, everyday level, we will unavoidably end up on the wrong path, replacing God's will with something else. "Seek first the Kingdom of God, and all these things shall be added to you" (Luke 12:31 NKJV).

When we pray that God's will might reign "on Earth as in Heaven," we should first and foremost be ready to follow His will ourselves. It is very unfortunate that we often identify obedience with the oppression of our personal freedom, mistakenly thinking that those who obey are enslaved and those who give obediences to others are the masters. In actuality, things are different. It is not only we who are called to listen to the will of God and to live in accordance with that will, to be obedient. The Lord Himself listens intently to each of our prayers and, one might say, fulfills an obedience. We ask Him for mercy and He gives it to us. We ask Him for forgiveness and He forgives us and helps us in the difficult moments of our lives.

All of the Divine Services that we participate in are nothing other than the Lord's own ceaseless obedience to mankind, starting with His obedience to death, and death on the Cross (Phil. 2:8). That was His chief act of obedience, obedience not only to God the Father but also to all mankind.

"Give us this day our daily bread..."

Turning to God with this request, we are, of course, asking for everything that we consider necessary for life. In Greek, the word is ἐπιούσιος, the meaning of which is a little obscure, but which can mean "essential" or "necessary." In English, we say "daily bread," which gives the petition an emphatically day-to-day kind of meaning.

When we pray to God not to leave us without His care and to give us bread for sustenance, by "bread" we understand the entirety of what is necessary for life. In the Sermon on the Mount, Jesus instructs His disciples:

> "Do not be anxious about your life, what you will eat or what you will drink, nor about your body, what you will put on. Is not life more than food, and the body more than clothing? Look at the birds of the air: they neither sow nor reap nor gather into barns, and yet your Heavenly Father feeds them. Are you not of more value than they? And which of you by being anxious can add a single hour to his span of life? And why are you anxious about clothing? Consider the lilies of the field, how they grow: they neither toil nor spin, yet I tell you, even Solomon in all his glory was not arrayed like one of these. But if God so clothes the grass of the field, which today is alive and tomorrow is thrown into the oven, will he not much more clothe you, O you of little faith? Therefore do not be anxious, saying, 'What shall we eat?' or 'What shall we drink?' or 'What shall we wear?' For the Gentiles seek after all these things, and your Heavenly Father knows that you need them all. But

seek first the Kingdom of God and His righteousness, and all these things will be added to you" (Matthew 6:25-33).

The Lord said to the Jews:

"I am the Bread of Life. Your fathers ate the manna in the wilderness, and they died. This is the Bread that comes down from Heaven, so that one may eat of it and not die. I am the Living Bread that came down from Heaven. If anyone eats of this Bread, he will live forever. And the Bread that I will give for the life of the world is My Flesh. <...> Truly, truly, I say to you, unless you eat the Flesh of the Son of Man and drink His blood, you have no life in you. Whoever feeds on My Flesh and drinks My Blood has eternal life, and I will raise him up on the last day. For My Flesh is true food, and My Blood is true drink. Whoever feeds on My Flesh and drinks My Blood abides in Me, and I in him" (John 6:48-56).

When we have thought deeply about these teachings of the Lord, we will begin to understand the Lord's Prayer in a completely different way. The Lord's Prayer is not just a request for earthly good things. Its true, deeper meaning is opened for us through the words of Holy Scripture, "Man shall not live by bread alone, but by every word that comes from the mouth of God" (Matt. 4:4).

In Greek, the word ἐπιούσιος simultaneously means "urgent," or necessary for existence, and "that which is above all essence," super-essential. The Holy Fathers of the Church interpret this prayer for bread in a deeply spiritual and Eucharistic sense. It is no accident that the Lord's Prayer is sung at Liturgy right before communion of Christ's Holy Mysteries—the Lord's Prayer is a Eucharistic prayer. In this prayer, we ask for the Bread of Life.

"And forgive us our trespasses as we forgive those who trespass against us…"

FForgive us like we forgive others. Remit our transgressions to the same extent that we forgive those who have trespassed against us. Or to turn the meaning of the prayer the other way around: "Do not forgive us since we do not forgive those who trespass against us."

We can keep strict fasts, read our morning and evening prayers consistently, do good works, help our neighbors, and strive to please God in everything, but as soon as we say these words and are unable to forgive someone something, we cross out everything that we've accomplished with all that work. All of it instantly becomes meaningless and turns to dust.

One might think, "Yes, I'm a sinner, but I can do something good that will cover some of my sin." But it turns out that the one thing that can justify us is not the collection of our good works, not our generosity in giving, not the number of prayers that we read, but our ability and desire to forgive.

When it comes down to it, forgiving is not easy. Often, a person would be happy to forgive but cannot manage it. It is a very complicated, spiritual process. But the Lord, like always, is merciful. Even when we cannot forgive, He's ready to accept our intention, our striving to follow the path of forgiveness. The most important thing for us is not to back down.

"And lead us not into temptation..."

People often understand the word "temptation" in at least two different ways. First of all, we are used to thinking of temptation as some kind of external pressure, pushing us onto the path of sin. Quite often we ascribe to temptation what is actually the fruit of our own free will, heart, and mind. "Well, it was so tempting!" we repeat in such situations.

This has become almost a proverb for us Orthodox and it is silly. We are ready to see temptation everywhere but we should not discount our own inherent desire to live exclusively for ourselves, looking at those around us only as some kind of annoying hindrance in achieving this, as we try to find in them qualities that would allow us to justify in our own eyes our own unworthiness. We see in this the depth of our fall from God, and temptation has nothing to do with it.

However, true temptations do exist. Satan tempts the Lord in the desert after His baptism. He tempts Him as a man since God cannot be tempted. And even now, humanity is tormented by the same three temptations. The demon says to Christ, who has fasted for forty days in the wilderness, "Command these stones to become loaves of bread" (Matt. 4:3).

It happens that it is now within our human power to turn what is lifeless into a source of earthly goods. The modern processes that feed us all are, strictly speaking, those loaves that have become bread for us. Man has become a great consumer. Consumer rights are ranked as a kind of new morality. People consume each other and everything around them.

The Lord teaches us how we should answer this temptation: "Man shall not live by bread alone, but by every word that comes from the mouth of God" (Matt. 4:4). And in the Sermon on the Mount, He instructs His disciples, saying, "Seek first the Kingdom of God and His righteousness, and all these things will be added to you" (Matt. 6:33).

"Then the devil took him to the holy city and set him on the pinnacle of the temple and said to him, 'If You are the Son of God, throw yourself down, for it is written, "He will command His angels concerning You," and "On their hands they will bear You up, lest You strike Your foot against a stone."' Jesus said to him, 'Again it is written, "You shall not put the Lord your God to the test"'" (Matt. 5:5-7).

We are all familiar with this temptation, too. "Look at the world that lies before you! Let's soar! Let's throw restraint aside and give in to our desires! We have absolute, unhindered freedom! We can do whatever we want! There are no ethics, no moral criteria, there is only freedom!" The tragedy, however, is that behind that freedom, there is a hidden abyss and at the bottom of it—inescapable death.

"Again, the devil took Him to a very high mountain and showed Him all the kingdoms of the world and their glory. And he said to Him, 'All these I will give You, if You will fall down and worship me.' Then Jesus said to him, 'Be gone, Satan! For it is written, "You shall worship the Lord your God and

Him only shall you serve"'" (Matt. 4:8-10).

We will leave this last bit without comment. It speaks for itself. Soon or later, these three temptations come to each of us.

The other meaning of the word "temptation" is a trial or a test. We consider people to be "tried and tested" when they have gone through trials with dignity and have truly mastered their craft. As an aside, in ancient times, when rocks that contained gold were melted, that was also called a "trial" of the gold.

With this kind of "temptation," it is God Himself who is testing us. We find examples of this kind of "temptation" in the Holy Scriptures. In the Book of Genesis, we read about how the Lord tempted Abraham. Abraham's long-awaited son Isaac was born. However, God told him to offer his child up as a burnt offering. Abraham loaded his son with a bundle of wood and they began to climb the mountain not far from Golgotha. Traditionally, this is thought to have taken place on the spot where Omar's Mosque now stands. Isaac kept asking, "Where are we going? Where is the lamb for the burnt offering?" not understanding that he himself was the lamb. Abraham answered him, "The Lord Himself will send the lamb." Abraham, who had been promised by God Himself that it was through Isaac that his seed would be blessed and multiply like the sand of the sea, like the stars of Heaven, went to fulfill the will of God. He bound his son's hands and feet and raised the knife for the sacrifice and then an angel appeared and freed Isaac, replacing him with a lamb.

From then on, Abraham has been called the father of those who believe. Why? Because his faith was shown not only in his knowledge that God exists and that we should bring Him sacrifices; it was shown not only in the fact that he followed God's will implicitly; rather, his faith was also shown in how he believed in God, that He is able to combine in Himself seemingly contradictory things, without hesitation fulfilling two seemingly contradictory promises.

20

AFTER THE LORD'S PRAYER:
HOLY THINGS ARE FOR THE HOLY

After the "Our Father" (which is the final Eucharistic prayer) has been sung, the priest reads the "Prayer at the Bowing of the Heads." "Peace be unto all! Bow your heads unto the Lord," and then imparts the blessing to the faithful. The parishioners bow their heads and the priest prays in the Altar, "We give thanks unto Thee, O King invisible. Who by Thy measureless power hast made all things, and in the multitude of Thy mercy hast brought all things from nothing into being. Do Thou Thyself, O Master, look down from Heaven upon those who have bowed their heads unto Thee; for they have not bowed down unto flesh and blood, but to Thee, the terrible God. Therefore, O Master, do Thou Thyself distribute these gifts here spread forth, unto all of us for good, according to the individual need of each: voyage with those who sail by sea and air; journey with those who travel by land; heal the sick, Thou who art the physician of our souls and bodies ..."

In this prayer, the priest asks God for His earthly blessings, that He would send each of us what we need. The people can no longer think about their own needs because they are thinking of God and the priest is interceding on their behalf, asking that in addition to their search for the Kingdom of Heaven and for His righteousness, "all these things" would also be added to them (Matt. 6:33).

The prayer ends with the exclamation, "Through the grace and compassion and love toward man of Thine Only-begotten Son ..." to which the choir responds "Amen." At this moment, the normal practice is to close the curtain of the Royal Doors. The priest reads the prayer for the breaking of the Bread and for the receiving of the Eucharist: "Look down, O Lord Jesus Christ, our God, from Thy holy dwelling-place ..." in which he asks God to grant him and all those serving with him (in other words, all those present in the church) His Body and Blood: "... and vouchsafe by Thy mighty hand to impart unto us Thine immaculate Body and precious Blood, and through us unto all the people."

Standing in front of the Holy Doors, the deacon rearranges his orarion in the shape of a cross, symbolizing his readiness to serve the Holy Eucharist, and then along with the priest, he says "O God, cleanse me a sinner, and have mercy on me," three times.

Seeing the priest stretching out his hand to the Lamb, the deacon exclaims, "Let us attend!" in other words, let us pay complete attention. The deacon encourages the worshipers to stand reverently and then he enters the Altar. The priest takes the Holy Lamb in his hands, elevates it high above the Diskos, and says, "The Holy Things are for the holy!"

During the Communion of the Clergy, the Altar is an image of the Upper Room in which the apostles received Holy Communion with their Teacher.

* * *

"The Holy Things are for the holy" is the exclamation that rings out at the end of Liturgy before the faithful come up to the Chalice. The Church proclaims that the Holy Things will now be given to the holy—that is, to each of us. It is important to understand that on the one hand, the Lord calls each of us present there in the temple to holiness and on the other hand, He sees holiness in each of us and considers each of us to be holy because the Body and Blood of Christ can only be given to the holy, only the holy can have communion with God and not be destroyed by the fire of divinity. The entrance into the Kingdom of Heaven is only opened to those who are holy. And it is precisely during the Eucharist that the Heavenly Gates are opened.

The Church answers on behalf of all the faithful, "One is holy, one is Lord, Jesus Christ, to the glory of God the Father." These words are full of repentance and contrition of heart. "No one who is bound with the desires and pleasures of flesh is worthy ..." the priest reads during the singing of the Cherubic Hymn.

We cannot allow ourselves not to strive for holiness. The Liturgy does not leave us any other possibility—it reminds each of us who we are, what the Lord calls us to, and who we should become. Each of us once again receives that same great task that we were given in Holy Baptism. We should not be afraid of the fact we are intended to be saints. We should desire it with all of our hearts and apply the word "The Holy Things are for the holy" to ourselves.

21
COMMUNION OF THE CLERGY AND FAITHFUL

The deacon enters the Altar and turns to the priest who has already placed the Lamb on the Diskos and says, "Divide, Master, the Holy Bread." The priest once again takes the Lamb and breaks It in the form of a Cross into four pieces, with the words, "Divided and distributed is the Lamb of God, Who is divided, yet not disunited; Who is ever eaten yet not consumed, but sanctifies those who partake thereof ..."

As you may recall, the Lamb is stamped with the name of Christ and the word "NIKA," which means "victory." The portion of the lamb with the inscription "IC" (meaning "Jesus") is placed at the top of the Diskos. At the bottom of the Diskos is placed the portion with the inscription "XC" (meaning Christ).

The top part of the Lamb is called "the Pledge." During the sacrament of Ordination, the newly ordained priest approaches the Holy Table. The bishop takes the Pledge and places it in the priest's hands with the words, "Receive thou this pledge, and preserve it whole and unharmed until thy last breath, because thou shalt be held to an accounting therefore in the Second and Awesome Coming of our Great Lord, God, and Savior, Jesus Christ." The priest holds it over the Altar for the rest of the service as a pledge of priesthood, a pledge of the most important thing that the priest will do in his life—serve Liturgy and turn the people of God to Christ. He will have to give an account for that on the fearful day of the Last Judgment.

When the Lamb has been divided and placed on the Diskos, the priest places the Pledge into the Chalice and says, "The fullness of the Cup, of the Faith, of the Holy Spirit." Afterward, the deacon brings warm water (the Zeon), exclaiming, "Bless, Master, the Zeon," and pours it into the Chalice with the words, "The warmth of faith, full of the Holy Spirit. Amen."

This is a necessary condition for communion in the Holy Mysteries of Christ. The Zeon is important. First of all, in a traditional sense, because in the ancient world, people never drank undiluted wine. It was thought that only barbarians would drink wine that way. Additionally, undiluted wine can make a person cough, especially if it's cold. Finally, though, the Zeon is a symbol of the warmth of human faith.

* * *

The priest and the deacon bow before the Throne. They ask forgiveness from each other and from all the people present in the temple and reverently commune first of the Body and then of the Blood of the Savior.

Ordinarily, while the clergy are communing, the choir sings spiritual hymns or reads prayers before Communion. The parishioners should listen to these prayers with piety and contrition of heart, preparing themselves to receive the Holy Mysteries of Christ.

※ ※ ※

After this, the portion of the Lamb with the inscription "NIKA," which is intended for the communion of the laity, is broken into pieces. This is accompanied by the words of the prayer, "Having beheld the Resurrection of Christ ..." The priest takes the spear in his hands and carefully divides the Lamb on a special plate. The little particles are then carefully put into the Chalice which is then covered by a communion cloth.

The Diskos, with the particles that were taken out during the Proskomedia, remains on the Holy Table. It has the particles that were taken out in honor of the Theotokos, John the Forerunner, the apostles, hierarchs, etc.

"With the fear of God, and faith draw near ..." Usually, babies receive Communion first, without a large particle of the Body. The faithful piously receive the Holy Gifts, kissing the edge of the Chalice. Kissing the Chalice is symbolic of touching the risen Savior, feeling Him and verifying the truth of His Resurrection. According to some commentators on the Liturgy, the edge of the Chalice symbolizes Christ's side.

It's worth remembering the text from the Gospel:

"Now Thomas, one of the twelve, called

the Twin, was not with them when Jesus came. So the other disciples told him, 'We have seen the Lord.' But he said to them, 'Unless I see in his hands the mark of the nails, and place my finger into the mark of the nails, and place my hand into His side, I will never believe.' Eight days later, his disciples were inside again, and Thomas was with them. Although the doors were locked, Jesus came and stood among them and said, 'Peace be with you.' Then he said to Thomas, 'Put your finger here, and see My hands; and put out your hand, and place it in My side. Do not disbelieve, but believe.' Thomas answered him, 'My Lord and my God!' Jesus said to him, 'Have you believed because you have seen Me? Blessed are those who have not seen and yet have believed'" (John 20:24–29).

* * *

The most important thing happens when the Savior touches us—we enter into the Kingdom of Heaven. But we are filthy, unclean, and impure in the depth of our heart. Man can be very wicked, but that is how Christ accepts us.

But how can the Lord touch us? Only through His Crucifixion. He can only call us to follow Him. And in human terms, there's nothing pleasant or joyful in this because when the Lord touches you in His suffering, it is painful. In that moment, the Lord allows you to feel Him, to see Him, and to be with Him in that suffering. And that is very, very difficult, although that is why we come to church, why we have gathered together for Communion. But which of us has the strength to deny himself completely, to cross out his whole life and follow the Lord to the end, like He commands? Who can say that he is ready to give up everything for Christ's sake and the Gospel's (cf. Mark 8:35)? Are we truly ready for that? Questions like that don't have an answer. This likely isn't within human power to accomplish.

Our humanity rises in revolt against this idea and protests, "How is it possible to forget about everything? How can we willingly give up everything?" A strange thing happens. On the one hand, we bow down before the Life-creating Cross, we have been baptized in the name of Christ, in order to take up that cross, to carry it and to be co-crucified with the Lord. On the other hand, we're not strong enough to actually do that. But we can't do anything else. The word has already been spoken, we've made our vows to God and there is no way back.

Our souls are caught in state of terrible dichotomy. The Savior calls us to follow Him and we resist His call and are miserable, unable to make up our mind. We live in this state. We come to church in this weak, completely helpless state. And then we commune in the Holy Mysteries of Christ and ask God to heal our souls and bodies, to strengthen our will, to help us realize our potential, to make us into the people that He wishes us to be. Because it's not within our power to be true Christians, not within our power to fulfill the Gospel. We need to grasp this concept. We cannot fulfill the Gospel. Christianity is above human ability. That which Christ demands of us we are unable to do. That is why the world has never understood Christianity.

However, the Savior comes and gives us Himself when we receive His Holy Mysteries. And what used to be impossible for us human beings now becomes possible. Something great and terrible happens. Man is joined to the same Cross that he was so afraid of. We commune in the Lord's Blood and if we trust Him completely, He will guide us after Himself.

We should receive Communion with the thought, "Lord, I'm ready to go with You even to Golgotha!" And then He gives us that great joy of abiding with Him to the very end.

* * *

After communion, the choir sings, "Alleluia," and the priest goes into the Altar and places the Chalice on the Holy Table. The deacon takes the Diskos in his hands and brushes the particles that were left on it into the Chalice with the words, "Wash away, O Lord, the sins of all those commemorated here, by Thy precious Blood: through the prayers of Thy saints."

That is the completion of the commemoration of the living and the dead, who are immersed in the death and Resurrection of Christ. The Chalice, with the particles submerged in it, in this case symbolizes how the Lord took on Himself the sins of the world, washed them away by His Blood, redeemed us by His crucifixion, death, and Resurrection and gave us Eternal Life.

The words "... through the prayers of all Thy saints" don't just refer to the saints who are commemorated on that day, although of course we do seek their graceful aid. In this case, however, we're speaking about all of the Christians who are gathered together in the temple. In other words, it is through the Blood of Christ and the prayers of the Holy Church that sins are washed away and forgiven. That is precisely why liturgical prayer is universal and all-powerful.

After the particles are immersed in the Chalice, the Chalice is covered by a Communion cloth. The other cloths, as well as the spoon and the star, are put on the Diskos. The priest turns and faces the people and, blessing them, says, "O Lord, save Thy people and bless Thine inheritance." The choir responds, "We have seen the True Light, we have received the Heavenly Spirit, we have found the true faith, worshiping the undivided Trinity Who has saved us."

While "We have seen the true light ..." is being sung, the priest carries the Diskos to the prothesis table, as he quietly reads the prayer, "Be Thou exalted, O God, above the Heavens, and Thy glory above all the Earth," in memory of our Lord Jesus Christ's bodily ascent into Heaven and our own future ascent into Heaven, when we have been deified by grace. This moment in the Liturgy once again emphasizes mankind's true calling, the higher purpose of our earthly life.

Notice that all the laws of nature act downward, pulling us lower, like the law of gravity. Everything on Earth "falls"—rain, snow, hail ... We even call the world itself "fallen." But Christ, having ascended to Heaven, annuls the inevitability of the laws of this fallen world. He shows us that through communion with God, man overcomes this earthly gravity.

Knowing about all of our weaknesses, about our tendency to sin and how we don't strive for spiritual life, the Lord nevertheless raises up our human nature that He has taken on Himself. Mankind is given the gift of living free from the laws of the fallen world, hurrying upward. A Christian has no other way.

The priest censes the Holy Gifts and, bowing before them, takes the Chalice in his hands with the words, "Blessed is our God ..." and then turns and faces the people and says, "always, now and ever, and unto ages of ages," reminding them of the Savior's promise to abide in His Church to the end of the age.

22

THANKSGIVING

The last part of Liturgy consists of thanksgiving for Communion and a dismissal blessing.

The choir sings, "Let our mouths be filled with Thy praise, O Lord ..." and the deacon exits the Altar for the last litany, a litany of thanksgiving, which begins with the words, "Stand upright! Having partaken ..." The command to "stand upright" reminds us that we should stand with piety, lifting our hearts to God.

At this point, the priest folds the antimension, takes the Gospel book and, making the sign of the Cross with it over the Holy Table, says, "For Thou art our sanctification, and unto Thee we ascribe glory ..." Then he exits the Altar to read the "Prayer behind the Ambo." "Let us depart in peace ... O Lord, who blessest those who bless Thee."

The choir sings, "Blessed be the name of the Lord, henceforth and forever ..." and then Psalm 33, "I will bless the Lord at all times ..."

The priest then gives the dismissal (which in Greek is called the ἀπόλυσις, the blessing for the worshipers to leave the temple at the end of the service): "May He who rose again from the dead, Christ our true God ..." and having blessed the people with the sign of the Cross, he then holds it out for them to kiss. Usually, while the faithful are kissing the Cross, Prayers of Thanksgiving after Communion are read. Then, having blessed the faithful again with the sign of the Cross, the priest goes back into the Altar, closes the Royal Gates, and pulls the curtain shut.

* * *

The Divine Service is finished. But what is a Divine Service? At first glance, the answer seems obvious. Christians come to Church to serve God. But if we really think deeply about this expression, then we will notice that really, it's hard to say who is serving whom. Like many words and expressions that the Church uses, the expression "Divine Service" has a double meaning.

What takes place during the Divine Service is what Christ accomplished at the Mystical Supper. Then, He gathered His apostles, took a basin of water, and began to wash their dirty feet with love, meekness, and humility. He washed the feet of each of them, even the traitor, even the one who would soon betray Him. That is an icon of true Divine Service—God serves His disciples. When we gather in church, the Lord washes all of our feet.

Oftentimes, we tell our children that they have to do this or that, but we ourselves don't do what we tell them to do. But the Lord showed us through His own example what we should do and how we should do it. As soon as we begin to get ready to approach

Him, He already begins to wash our feet.

From time to time, it seems to us like when we go to church, it's some kind of spiritual accomplishment on our part. After all, we waited in line for Confession, wrote out commemoration lists ... It never occurs to us that when we come to church, we are invisibly transported to the Upper Room, where the Lord washed His disciples' feet and that now it's our turn.

We turn to God and ask for His help and right away He begins to serve us, fulfilling our trifling desires, helping us solve our everyday problems. We go to Confession and He once again serves us, washing the filth from us. Who serves whom at the Divine Liturgy? After all, it is the Lord who gives us His Body and His Blood! He is the one that is engaged in service to us.

The same thing is true about all of the Mysteries of the Church. They all contain the image of the Lord washing our feet. That is what true Divine Service is. Everything that happens with us in the Church is God's own ceaseless service to mankind. The Heavens above serve us, with the Lord heading it all up. The Lord receives all who come to the Church and Himself serves the Divine Service as the great High Priest. He only expects one thing from us. He expects us to strive to become like Him.

Having washed His disciples' feet, Jesus commanded them, "If I then, your Lord and Teacher, have washed your feet, you also ought to wash one another's feet. For I have given you an example, that you also should do just as I have done to you" (John 13:14-15). We must at last understand—we fulfill our divine service when we serve our neighbor and when we truly, without hypocrisy, fulfill God's commandments.

And how else could we serve the Lord? What

else could God need from us? Our candles? Money? Prayers? Commemoration lists? Fasts? It goes without saying that God doesn't need anything. He only wants our deep, sincere, heartfelt love. It is when we manifest that love that we perform our divine service. When that love becomes the meaning of our life, then whatever we do will become service to God, a continuation of the Divine Liturgy.

The Divine Liturgy is the union of Divine Service and thanksgiving, where the Lord serves us and we serve Him. It is the common work of God and His people. It is in this union that the Church is manifested as a divine-human body. It is then that the Church becomes truly a universal event, a Church that is catholic and that cannot be overcome.

www.ingramcontent.com/pod-product-compliance
Lightning Source LLC
Chambersburg PA
CBHW030329100526
44592CB00010B/626